From Sleepwalking to Living!

Stop Feeding Narcissists, End People-Pleasing, and Take Back Your Life

By
Kate Howells

Terms and Conditions
LEGAL NOTICE

© Copyright 2025 ©**katehowells**

All rights reserved. The content contained within this book may not be reproduced, duplicated, or transmitted without direct written permission from the author or the publisher. Email requests to kevin@babystepspublishing.com

Under no circumstances will any blame or legal responsibility be held against the publisher or author for any damages, reparation, or monetary loss due to the information contained within this book, either directly or indirectly.

Legal Notice:

This book is copyright-protected. It is only for personal use. You cannot amend, distribute, sell, use, quote, or paraphrase any part of the content within this book without the consent of the author or publisher.

Disclaimer Notice:

Please note the information contained within this document is for educational and entertainment purposes only. All efforts have been executed to present accurate, up-to-date, reliable, and complete information. No warranties of any kind are declared or implied. Readers acknowledge the author is not engaging in the rendering of legal, financial, medical, or professional advice. The content within this book has been derived from various sources. Please consult a licensed professional before attempting any techniques outlined in this book.

By reading this document, the reader agrees under no circumstances is the author responsible for any losses, direct or indirect, that are incurred as a result of the use of the information contained within this document, including, but not limited to, errors, omissions, or inaccuracies.

Published by Babysteps Publishing Limited All enquires to kevin@babystepspublishing.com

ISBN- 9798287433246

Table of Contents

Why I Wrote This Book — 1
Why Should You Read This Book? — 5
Chapter 1 — 7
   Dissatisfied With Life? What Can be Done About it? — 7
Chapter 2 — 15
   I'm Traumatised. I Can't Help How I Feel, Right? — 15
Chapter 3 — 23
   I Can't Help Being an Anxious Person. Right? — 23
Chapter 4 — 31
   I Can't Help What I Think. Right? — 31
Chapter 5 — 39
   Narcissism - The What and The Why — 39
Chapter 6 — 47
   Why Am I a Magnet for Narcissists? — 47
Chapter 7 — 55
   Narcissistic Hangover: The Aftermath — 55
Chapter 8 — 65
   Why We Should Be Grateful to All Narcissists — 65
Chapter 9 — 75
   I Just Need to Love Myself. Right? — 75
Chapter 10 — 83
   Manifest. Can I Have It All? — 83
Chapter 11 — 91
   How Do I Know What I Want? — 91
Chapter 12 — 99
   BONUS CHAPTER — 99
   Reprogram Your Mind — 99

About the Author	107
Other Books and Services by the Author	109
One More Thing Before You Go…	111
Bibliography	113

Why I Wrote This Book

I decided to write this book for two reasons. The first is that I like to be really clear about how I work and had been wondering for some time what would be the most helpful way of doing that. I was writing content for my new website and I had written much more than I needed. Then, just at the right time, I received an email from Kevin Long at Babysteps Publishing, asking if I had considered writing a book about my business. This was exactly what I was looking for as a means of explaining what I do in an organised way. I signed up that week.

The second reason for writing this is that I feel there is an unpleasant trend in talking therapies in the UK currently. Trauma training is advertised everywhere a counsellor might look, with endless courses offering a myriad of tools to alleviate its effects. This has seeped into the counselling rooms and out the door with the clients. Staff in schools, health services and social services are also being trained to spot and manage trauma in those they support. As a result, vast numbers of people, both children and adults, are now referring to themselves as traumatised.

This is perfect fodder for newspapers and social media, filling pages of content—because trauma sells. As a result, I have noticed that professionals place more emphasis on the person seeking help being a victim. I don't see this as a healthy development but rather as one that is disempowering for the individual and unhelpful societally. It moves people away from taking responsibility for their actions.

This feels like a significant step backwards with regard to how the helping professions view those they are working with. In the early 20th century, Freud's drive theory of the person was extrapolated from mentally unwell patients. Years of psychoanalysis were considered necessary to help a person become, at best, less neurotic. In contrast, behaviourists, such as Watson, saw the person as nothing more than the sum of external stimuli. From both perspectives, the view of the person was bleak.

However, Maslow's humanistic approach emerged in the mid-20th century, describing a very different kind of human. Maslow's person was inherently good, primed for self-actualisation, a state possible for all as long as fundamental needs were first met. This person *was responsible* for making sense of and making meaning in their own life. Carl Rogers' Person-Centred Counselling was based on this premise, and watching him in videos, it is clear that he saw each client as their full potential. The Gestalt Therapy developed by Fritz Perls et al. also views the person as having the wherewithal to take responsibility for themselves and break free from maladaptive patterns of behaviour, should they wish to

Fast-forward to now, the twenty-first century, and the emphasis on trauma and 'these poor people'. Consequently, there is a lot of talk of 'It's not your fault', 'You don't have to forgive', 'You are a survivor'…. Whilst it is essential for people not to blame themselves for being abused by others, and this is an important part of recovery, this is only the start of the process. Staying at this stage means leading a limited life.

This is crucial, as most clients of all ages are now seeking counselling because of the effects of interactions with narcissists. This might be from parents, children, siblings, coworkers, bosses, friends or intimate relationships. A sea-change of this magnitude can have only one explanation: evolution. We are adapting as a species according to our beliefs and values, and one of the new means of surviving the current landscape is narcissism. If everyone affected by these behaviours adopts a victim identity, that mindset will only serve to shape society in a more disempowered and unhealthy direction.

The adaptation of people-pleasing is escalating to an equal degree to that of narcissism. The two responses are opposite sides of the same coin. Neither party is able to accept themselves, making their sense of worth entirely dependent on how others view them. Whilst social media has its benefits, it exerts a magnetic pull on anyone seeking validation outside of themselves. Not only does it attract narcissists and people-pleasers, but it also plays a role in creating them.

Narcissists will keep going until a non-negotiable boundary is put in and, unfortunately, a people-pleaser has been conditioned from childhood to have next to no boundaries. This creates the perfect environment for abuse. In the UK, there are endless articles, TV and radio programmes complaining that there is not enough help for traumatised people. There are countless forums, newspaper articles, blogs and posts about how awful narcissists are. While therapy is undoubtedly vital for recovery, it is not tackling the issue at its root. We need to make meaningful adjustments to how we live alongside narcissists **before** things reach crisis point.

Narcissists benefit from strong boundaries, and this helps them abuse less, which is ultimately better for them and better for others. When we abuse others, we cut ourselves with each attack on the other. In this book, I will be looking at how you might become more self-led. If you are a manipulator and you can begin to see that each time you control or hurt another you make your world smaller, that will be a result. If you are a people-pleaser and you begin to see that each time you allow yourself to be manipulated, you hurt yourself and benefit no one, then that will be a result. If you are an enabler, it will help you realise that you are not absolved of responsibility in this issue.

This isn't victim-blaming. This is educating ourselves to be able to stop seeking approval from others so that we can become more self-led.

Everything that I talk about in this book has been helpful to me and to many of my clients. You, too, might find it useful. Thank you for reading my book.

Why Should You Read This Book?

What am I going to tell you in this book that will make any difference to you? What is the point of reading on? There are so many self-help books with so many methods. How will this one differ? I am not going to tell you anything new. Everything has already been said countless times and many people have bookcases and apps full of it, myself included.

So, if I'm not telling you anything new, why should you read the book? Reading this book is going to help pass into you, as if by osmosis, the message that is behind every chapter. No, it isn't a subliminal message. I am going to tell you what the message is very clearly and repeat it over and over again. Here is the message: Unless you take full responsibility for yourself and for everything that happens to you, you will lead a limited life. You may resist this and want to stop reading now, but if you do read on and you do integrate the message into your being, you will not regret it.

You may have read countless self-improvement books, but unless you have read them from a vantage point that only you are responsible for all that happens in your life, it is unlikely you had results. All the methods are a waste of time unless you are doing them without lying to yourself. You are watching the Olympics from the stands and believing that will make you a medal winner. Reading countless books won't change you. Only you can do the work by realising you are the boss of your own life, no one else. Stop the denial or read fiction instead—you might enjoy it more.

In this book, I will be describing how you might sort out your own mind so that you are not controlled by others. I want to show how seeking the approval of others leaves you open to control. I don't mean just in your personal relationships, but by all of the junk you might be downloading from social media, the internet and news programmes. If you aren't in charge of your mind, someone else will be. As you begin to tidy up and take back charge of your mind, you will become more self-led, and your life will improve dramatically.

I would like you to see that you are not the sum of your experiences and that what has gone before need not define you. I would like you to feel as good as possible, and I hope that when you have finished this book, you will, at the very least, see that this is achievable. I would like you to see that you can start the process of letting go of the kind of thinking that is making you feel so mediocre. Freud (1929) said that people don't truly desire freedom because it necessitates the taking of responsibility for themselves. I would like you to see that it is worth taking responsibility for everything you have ever done and ever will do because that is the only route to freedom. The choice is yours and yours only.

Chapter 1

Dissatisfied With Life? What Can be Done About it?

You may have benefitted from therapy in the past, felt better for a while, but found that, generally, *you just don't feel that good.* Relationships may still be difficult for you; you might have a number of destructive habits that you can't let go of; you might be stuck in a dreary job and only coping with work because you have a holiday coming up soon. All of the above are extremely common, so is this as good as life gets? Is this all you should aspire to? If the present is so uninspiring, no wonder people believe and commonly say that it is important to have something to look forward to.

Up until I was about 9 years old, I believed there was more to life than the above. When I say believed, I mean I had no doubt because it hadn't occurred to me that grown-up life would be so dull. I believed that life would be exciting when I grew up, and I would have adventures like the 'Famous Five', finding secret passages and ingots of gold. My dad could rebuild a traction engine, and so I asked him to make me a broomstick that would fly. I believed it was possible. When I read stories about time travel, I assumed it could happen to anyone.

Gradually, the excitement waned as I succumbed to the widely held belief that one must accept one's limitations and lead a life of mediocrity. I became increasingly disappointed. As I grew older, I found the kinds of things people did to socialise boring. I felt trapped in the theatre and cinema. A party was only bearable with alcohol. I always had a partner because that is what I assumed one did with one's life. I was average at most things and went from job to job with the sole aim of earning a living. Sometimes, I would try to learn something interesting to change careers, but it seemed too difficult. I would slip back under the miserable veil.

It never occurred to me that it would be possible to take charge of the way I live my life so that I could begin to live it as I want to live it. The general viewpoint seems to be that if you are lucky, you are dealt a good hand, and if you are unlucky, life will be tough. The accepted trajectory: following school, go to university or get a job; have a family, if desired (biological or otherwise); work until retirement, praying you have enough to survive on. Life is a struggle, and then you die. Accept it sooner rather than later, or you will be disappointed. You might have what is referred to as a midlife crisis as you momentarily try to drag yourself out of your mediocre existence. It is less a crisis and more a case of thinking that surely there has to be more to life than you are experiencing. However, you will soon settle back down into what is expected of you. A life of riches and success is reserved for the few, and a life of drudgery and struggle for the masses.

If you are reading this book, you, like me, may have found yourself dissatisfied with this widely accepted view of adult life. If you are reading this book, you are not sufficiently cloaked in denial to have given up hope. There is life in the old dog yet. I don't feel it is unfair to say that most people live in denial, sleepwalking through life. If you can see that there is a choice regarding whether to sleepwalk or wake up, that is an opening in the veil, a way through. Eureka! This is good news indeed.

What will you have to do to wake up? I am afraid that the prescription is not a short one. To be awake and stay awake requires commitment and effort.

1. Deal with unresolved childhood issues - If you haven't already done so, get some therapy!

If you have not yet had counselling and are on the lookout for the first time, the variety of approaches on offer can seem overwhelming. Don't worry about the latest, most fashionable methods. They are only as good as the counsellor using them. My recommendation is to look at counsellors' photos on online directories and see if you could imagine yourself talking about you to that face.

You want to feel understood, ideally by a counsellor who can get down in the quagmire with you whilst keeping one foot firmly on the ground. If a counsellor overly identifies with the trauma, they can fail to see the potential for growth and beyond. Use the counsellor as an investigator to help you find out why you are acting as you are in the world now. This will indicate what has not been let go of from the past. As you let go of these unhelpful patterns, you can experiment with new and more beneficial behaviours.

The clues to what is getting in the way in the present can nearly always be linked to that which has occurred in childhood. Those who say they have had a perfect childhood never have, and the next question might be, 'Who could you go to when you were sad or had a problem?' They will answer that their family didn't really talk about feelings, but as they were well provided for in other ways, that was fine. Roughly translated: there was zero emotional support. In contrast, those who know they had a difficult childhood tend to more readily say that that they did so. However, both parties will usually say that it wasn't their parents' fault, and they don't want to blame them.

What helps here is to explain to them that admitting how it really was is essential and only the start of the process.

These are the important points that I cover:

I am very used to hearing all kinds of things about families and know that most are dysfunctional.

I don't want to gang up on the parents with them but to help them honestly see how it really was growing up.

To deny what happened and also say that they don't blame the parents is a riddle that can never be solved. This is why so many are stuck in this stage. If they are saying the parents didn't do anything wrong, then what are they saying they don't blame them for?

Whilst this stage of therapy is going on, they will probably feel a range of emotions, such as anger, anxiety and sadness.

There is no need to get stuck in the feelings. People worry that it is going to be endless sessions of being asked how they feel and the counsellor looking concerned. Sometimes it is enough to acknowledge the feelings to someone who understands.

It is crucial to fully and truthfully acknowledge how the parents affected them. Unless this part is properly dealt with, any further work will be hindered by self-blame and denial of the truth.

It is then time to look at why the parents might have acted as they did. This involves looking at what the parents' and grandparents' childhoods were like so that reasons, not excuses, for the behaviour become clearer.

It can then be possible to forgive the parents because it is clear that they were acting according to their own unresolved childhood issues. Freud said that what is left unsaid by the parents will be played out in the children (Hosein & Bulut, 2021). In experiments on generations of rats, unpleasant stimuli reacted to by one generation will be avoided by subsequent generations. In humans it will just keep coming on down the generations unless it is spoken of and released.

Forgiveness is not for the parent but for the client, so that they can free themselves from carrying this around. Forgiveness means not carrying into other relationships behaviours based on that which occurred years ago. Through this process, clients may also improve their relationship with their parents as they gain a deeper understanding of why their parents acted as they did.

I find that introducing this concept early on makes it easier to move through these stages. It is not about forcing forgiveness, but about offering a roadmap that transcends identification with the past. Some clients embrace this immediately and move through the stages quickly, while for others, it's more about keeping the roadmap in mind for reference. Without introducing this possibility, how would anyone know they have the potential to move beyond the past?

If you have grown up in a toxic environment, then toxic relationships seem completely normal. It is a bit like a fish being born in a stagnant pond. All of the other pond-life are suffering the negative effects of an unhealthy environment, and the limitations are just accepted. On the other side of the bank, there is a clear pond, home to all kinds of thriving life. The fish doesn't know that a clear pond is something that exists, let alone that it could be reached. It would be really helpful if someone at least showed the fish that the other pond was there. The fish is going to have to do some work to find its way through to the clear pond. Now it knows about the clear pond, it has a choice.

You, too, have a choice regarding what you look for in counselling. Do you want someone to challenge you, or do you want someone to comfort you? Do you want to keep going round in circles or start to push forward? People can waste a lot of money and time in counselling, justifying why they can't move on from whatever it is. Ideally, you have picked a counsellor who will challenge you on that in the way that I do. This will help you off the circular train track that you have been going round and round on all of your life so far. Once you realise that you can get off the train track, this is when you start taking responsibility for your life. This is when your life really begins to improve.

2. Clear out or update the jury in your mind.

In your mind resides a jury consisting of anyone towards whom you continue to feel guilt or resentment. Until you let go of the guilt and resentment, these people will inadvertently continue to shape your self-concept, affect your present-day relationships, negatively impact your self-worth and limit what you can and can't do. You will continue to project them on to every experience and person you meet, carrying your past into every present-day encounter. These corpses need moving on—their positions are redundant. If you want to be influenced by anyone, make sure that they have at least, the appropriate credentials.

This is a really interesting part of the work and clients will often find that the jury they are using in their mind to decide their success or failure is made up of people who are completely unsuitable for the task. For some, it might be the popular girl at school who wouldn't let them play; for others, the abusive ex; for many, the critical and shaming parent; for others, the bullying sibling; and for some, the person who shook their fist at them for driving too slowly 20 years ago. This might seem incredible, but it is this kind of motley crew that makes up the jury in our minds. What's more, many of them are long gone, and to most of them, **we** would be inconsequential. It's time to clear them out.

3. Wake up and understand you are not your thoughts.

You can change your life if you change your view of yourself. Negative thinking is addictive, considered the norm by the majority and like a slippery fish. If you talk to people you know about addressing the problem with this kind of work, they are likely to say it can't be done. They will try to keep you sleepwalking, just as they are. You will need to retrain yourself to stay awake and not slip back into the syrup.

4. Take responsibility for what is downloaded to your subconscious mind.

This is essential if you wish to live a better life. In a nutshell, your conscious mind is the master, and the subconscious is the genie in the lamp, unable to discern between fact and fiction. If, with your conscious mind, you are telling your subconscious that you are a loser, it will agree, 'Yes, master', and the genie will guide you towards the relevant experiences to make you lose in life. If you want to succeed in life and feel good, it is essential that your conscious mind gives the message to your subconscious that you are able to achieve and you can succeed in your life. *Your subconscious mind goes with what you believe,* not what you wish for.

Furthermore, if you are watching or listening to the news, reading newspapers and active on social media, you will be constantly exposed to negative information. If you are feeling low or anxious and have a pessimistic view of life, it is time to take a look at the kind of information you are exposing your subconscious mind to.

It is not only news and the internet that are negative. Most contemporary comedians base their acts on cynicism and self-deprecating humour. It must be what the majority want because it fills auditoriums. The masses are obsessed with film actors; however, when it comes to honouring the best at the Oscars, the world watches them being ridiculed and shamed during the ceremony. If you enjoy seeing those you admire being crushed, it might be time to ask yourself *just what is going on in your mind.*

5. Spring-clean your mind to make way for new possibilities. I want to help you see that you are not what you have experienced; you are not your trauma; you are nothing to do with who you have been told you are. As you clear out what you thought you were but are not, you will create space in your mind to be able to think about how you would like to be. If you are one of the many who have been using affirmations, meditation and visualisation to no avail, it is likely because for the rest and greater part of your day your thoughts have been negative. Your subconscious will accept the message it is hearing the most.

6. Bring in the power tool without which no one could start anything new—*the imagination.* You wouldn't be able to conceive of new ventures or possibilities without using your imagination. This isn't daydreaming. This is consciously imagining how you would like to lead your life.

The above six areas are going to be addressed in this book in a stepped approach.

In Chapter 2, we will be looking at the extent to which your perception of your childhood will determine your present-day life and how this might be addressed.

In Chapter 3, we will consider how you might change your perception of your anxiety. You can begin to take care of it rather than allowing it to run the show.

In Chapter 4, we will consider where your thoughts come from and whether you can do anything to manage them.

In Chapter 5, we will look at how childhood conditioning eases you into being controllable or controlling. We will look at why narcissism might develop as an adaptation.

In Chapter 6, we will address what it is about you that might make you a magnet or an enabler for narcissists.

In Chapter 7, we will look at the high cost of succumbing to the love-bombing of a narcissist.

In Chapter 8, we will consider why it is important to be grateful to all narcissists.

In Chapter 9, we will investigate how you might begin to direct yourself when you say no to being directed by others.

In Chapter 10, we will see how the law of attraction incorporates all of the aforementioned ideas for improving one's life.

In Chapter 11, we will look at whether it is possible to work out what we want with the mind that got us into this mess.

In Chapter 12, a bonus chapter, I describe an affirmation tool designed to help you reprogram your subconscious mind for success.

I love this work—let's get on with it!

.

Chapter 2

I'm Traumatised. I Can't Help How I Feel, Right?

In chapter one, I talked about the importance of therapy in addressing past or recent trauma. If someone has experienced deleterious relationships and events and never been listened to by someone who understood, it is likely that person will not feel good. Consequently, it can be said that how they feel is linked to the traumatic events inflicted upon them. However, in this chapter, I am going to explore whether you can help how you feel, even if you have had horrible experiences.

What I am now going to say will be unpalatable to some readers because it is the territory that tends to evoke responses such as 'victim-blamer'. However, I am not writing this book with the wish of me or it becoming popular—I am writing it to express what I have found out so far that works in improving how one experiences life, my own included. If what I am saying so far feels true to you, read on.

People perceive similar difficult life events in different ways. As such, some people who grow up in poverty are determined as adults to always have money, whereas others remain resigned to a lifetime of lack and struggle. Some people who have grown up in filth and squalor decide that they will never again live in such conditions, whereas others recreate them. The difference in the way that people perceive events is described beautifully in Shakespeare's Hamlet, 'For there is nothing either good or bad, but thinking makes it so'.

I find that, sometimes, although people have experienced a dismal childhood with abusive parents, they were aware, even at the time, that their parents were useless. They describe deciding at some point that this would not be the way that they would lead their adult lives. However, many others who have experienced dreadful upbringings inadvertently develop the defence of denial. Rather than see that their parents were not capable, they instead formed a self-concept of the unlovable child. This leads to an adulthood of confusion, self-loathing and difficulty managing both relationships and day-to-day living. You will know people who fit both categories here, and I think this will help you see that similar experiences are perceived in strikingly different ways. It is the person's perception, then, that will determine how good or bad the person feels, *not* the past events.

French psychologist Alice Miller, in *The Drama of Being a Child* (1987), describes why many abused children develop a false perception regarding their parents. Due to the pain being too overwhelming to process alone and there being no safe outlet for the expression of anger, the memories are repressed. Consequently, it is possible to continue to idolise the parent. Unfortunately, this usually continues into adulthood so that the person gets caught in a circular internal argument of *I hate them, but they're my parents, so I should love them*. Miller argues that love is earned, and if the parents have not been loving, why would or should the child feel love for them?

Miller describes this impasse as the basis for all mental health issues. In order to be set free, it is essential to recognise the abuse and neglect and know that the parent was at fault. Discussing the family system in which the parent was raised is also essential so that there is an explanation, not an excuse, for them having been so neglectful and incapable of giving love. Letting go of the hope that this adult will magically become a good parent helps put a stop to continuing to lay oneself open to more abuse from the parent in adulthood.

So, we can see from this that there is good reason for many people to have developed this enduring denial so early in life.

However, unless the denial is dropped and a more accurate version of the parent and past is accepted, there is no moving forward in any meaningful way. It is very difficult to accept that one's parents are incapable of being loving. However, American motivational speaker Wayne Dyer's (2013) explanation regarding this is helpful. He said that if you squeeze an orange, you won't get apple juice. He said that, in the same way, however hard you try to get love out of someone who has no access to love, it can't be done. It doesn't matter how hard you try. It isn't going to happen. **It has nothing to do with you being unlovable and everything to do with their ability to love being blocked.**

What we have been discussing here is the confusion many people feel having received inadequate parenting. *I hate him, but he's my dad. I hate her, but she's my mum….* However, this circular argument about parents occurs in subtler circumstances, which may not be recognised as abusive or neglectful. Your parents may never have hit you or raged at you; however, they may have conditioned you to accept abuse in your adult relationships with sarcasm, jokes at your expense and ridicule. Unfortunately, those having grown up in this kind of household seldom realise there is any issue with it. All verbal abusers start with these kinds of put-downs, and someone raised in a family relating in this way will not even question it. They are primed for abuse.

Your parents may have been functioning and seemed very capable, but the message may have been clear that love was directly related to how you behaved and what you achieved. If you failed that exam or lost that race, you were aware of their disappointment in you, whether it was overtly or covertly expressed. You may have internalised that as a model for all future relationships. That model is one of *'love is withdrawn if I don't succeed/conform/obey'.*

This form of conditional love is played out on social media daily. Posting congratulatory messages about one's children for achieving a degree, passing a driving test, winning a race, or completing a marathon is considered the norm. The word pride will be central to all of these posts, suggesting in some way that the achievement had anything to do with the parent, when often the result is despite the parent's influence. In therapy, I ask clients what this thing called pride is. I ask if they would post a gushing message about how proud they were of their child if they were battling drug addiction or psychosis. Pride is conditional and denotes ownership—it is self-aggrandisement and has nothing to do with love.

For the child who has been brought up by seemingly loving parents but is clear in the knowledge that failure to fulfil the parents' dream could mean withdrawal of that love, pride continues that sense of duty to please others. As long as your child is entangled in that web, they are not free and will be vulnerable to control by others as they aim to please.

If any of this resonates with you, what then can be done about it? If what happened in childhood is contributing to making you feel so bad, why not just blame your parents? Unfortunately, this will make you feel worse. As long as you are blaming anyone for anything, you will continue to argue with them in your mind and this will hold you back. The only way forward is to accept it happened and let it go. The events have been and gone, and they only live on in your memory, coloured by your perception. As such, no one else can sort this out. No one can help how you feel, not even those who were responsible for what happened to you. **Therefore, there is only one person with any chance of helping you feel good and that is you.**

If it is your perception of these experiences that will determine how good or bad you feel, is there anything you can do with that? Is there another way of viewing difficult experiences? Could there be any benefit to having experienced trauma? You may feel anger in response to that question. However, if you think about those you know who have been through turmoil, some will have said that it precipitated a positive change in their lives.

What could be the reason for people saying that adverse events have made them stronger? If we knew that, we could replicate their methods and we might feel good too. If we look specifically at the example of abuse, it is experienced at the hands of another/others. While we see ourselves as the helpless victims, there is the fear that we can't do anything to protect ourselves from abusers in the future. In order to feel anxiety-free about the future, I must believe that I can look after myself. If I was a helpless child when the abuse happened, how do I understand that in such a way that I feel I can handle myself moving forward?

In Chapter 1, I described the roadmap that I use to explain how recovery might be navigated and how far it might go. Here, I am going to suggest a route out of the internal conflict regarding blame of self and blame of the other. Many abusers have a sense of entitlement and no shame, so that the child takes on the shame. This can lead to a lifelong internal battle for the recipient of the abuse, one of oscillating between feeling that they should have been able to stop it and knowing it wasn't their fault. For some, this roadmap can be navigated straight away, but for others, being able to return to this as a concept throughout the therapy is really helpful.

Roadmap for dealing with self-blame:

1. I accept that I was a child, and it was not my fault.

2. I accept that it was the fault of the person who chose to abuse me/parent/s who had no love within them.

3. I accept that I cannot change the past.

4. Only I am in charge of my perception, and I now choose to no longer see myself as the victim of that person/parent/s.

5. I don't want that person living on in my mind. I don't need to be arguing with them in my head. They are responsible for what they did, and that is all I need to know.

6. I feel stronger because I know that I am the one who chooses who resides in my mind, and I don't choose that person.

7. I take full responsibility for how I perceive the past and present. As such, only I am in charge of my own life.

8. It's okay if I don't get this straight away—I just need to know that I can work towards taking back ownership of who resides in my mind.

If it is a situation that you walked into and ignored the warning signs, such as an adult abusive relationship, the prescription might look like this:

1. I admit to myself that I saw warning signs and chose to ignore them.

2. I celebrate the fact that I know I ignored the warning signs. This means I really know what the warning signs are.

3. I am an expert in recognising the warning signs and ignoring them.

4. I now choose to progress to being an expert in recognising the warning signs, acknowledging them and acting on them.

5. I am grateful to the abusive ex-partner/s for teaching me this skill.

6. I cut loose the abusive ex-partner/s from my mind and let them go on down the river. They have nothing more to teach me.

Once responsibility for your actions or perception of events is firmly taken back, things will begin to change for you. You will begin to see life from a different vantage point and will feel more in charge of how you feel. What others are up to will have less impact on your feelings. You will hold the remote control to your mind and body. Unless you are holding the remote control to your mind and body, somebody else will be. In fact, everyone will be passing around your remote control in a free-for-all unless you take it back.

I see it often in the counselling room when a client realises that they have allowed themselves to be controlled by another/others for their whole life. It is disturbing to realise that life could have been very different. This leads to the rewinding and playing back of life so far, investigating which controller held the remote control at which stage of the story. If you do this yourself, you will discover just how many people you have handed over control to in your life. When you do this, it is essential that you do it as an observer of your life so far. This will help prevent you from dropping down into self-criticism and despair.

You are now realising that you have been controlled for your whole life by perhaps parents, ex-partners, colleagues and friends. Prescription for changing your perception of this to work for you:

1. I have been controlled by others for my whole life.

2. I have previously been in denial of this fact, but now I fully realise it.

3. They are responsible for their controlling behaviours.

4. I am responsible for allowing them to have controlled me.

5. I celebrate the fact that I have allowed myself to be controlled and woken up to that fact.

6. This means I am an expert in recognising what being controlled feels like.

7. I will now become an expert in recognising and rejecting controlling behaviour.

8. If someone is telling me that I want to do something even though I know I don't, I will know that this is a sign of controlling behaviour. If I feel a push and pull in my body, a tightening in the gut, and a change in breathing, I will listen to these warning signs. I will say no because I hold the remote control, no one else.

For some clients, understanding that there is a choice regarding how we perceive and, therefore, feel about events and relationships, including those with ourselves, sparks a change within them. Rather than seeing it as victim-blaming, they see it as taking responsibility for themselves. When we take back responsibility, we also take back our power. When we blame others for how we feel, we are often left longing for an apology or retribution, believing that we can't let go until that happens. Unfortunately, many people who dish out abuse aren't ever sorry. It is helpful to recognise this and forget about receiving an apology or hearing of the abuser's comeuppance. It might never happen. You could be waiting your whole life for nothing.

In this chapter, we have investigated whether you can help how you feel when you have experienced traumatic events in the past. We have seen that you can, indeed, change how you perceive the past and yourself and that this makes a difference to how you feel. However, there are many other factors that contribute to the way you feel, and we will be looking at those in subsequent chapters, starting with how you can deal with anxiety in Chapter 3.

Chapter 3

I Can't Help Being an Anxi Person. Right?

When I trained as a counsellor, we were taught about trauma responses, in particular regarding anxiety, according to Maclean's Triune Brain Theory, developed in the 1960s (The Brain from Top to Bottom, n.d.). You may not know the name of the theory but will probably be familiar with the term 'lizard brain' as it is taught in schools, by coaches, therapists of all kinds, psychology text books and self-help books.

This theory proposed that the human brain evolved in three distinct stages. The earliest layer, referred to as the 'reptilian brain', was said to control basic life functions such as heart rate, breathing, and instinctual behaviour. Next to develop was the surrounding 'mammalian brain', the limbic system, responsible for emotional processing, learning, and memory. The most recent addition, the neocortex, enables language, abstract thought, and imagination.

Using this model, the understanding of anxiety, for instance, has been that our hunter-gatherer ancestors, in common with all animals, relied on the fight/flight/freeze response to evade predators. The part of the brain seen as responsible for sensing danger, the amygdala, prompted cortisol and adrenaline to be pumped around the body, leading to increased heart rate, blood pressure and breathing rate. This could be sustained for up to 30 minutes and increased the ability to run away from the threat, fight it or freeze if necessary.

Fast-forward to the 21st century and our sedentary office-based lifestyles, when this kind of response is often disproportionate to the threats we now face. If the amygdala kick-starts the same level of reaction every time the boss comes into the room as it once would

, in the presence of a lion, the effects will obviously be debilitating. According to the triune brain theory, when the prefrontal cortex is working optimally, it can restore calm by reasoning that it's only the boss—*not* a life-threatening predator (unless, of course, the boss is an actual danger!). However, for those with anxiety, the amygdala is said to fire indiscriminately, and the prefrontal cortex struggles to intervene and regulate the response. The connection is broken.

This theory has also been used to explain addiction, impulsivity, predatory sexual behaviours, anger outbursts, selfishness and other antisocial or maladaptive patterns. The understanding is that the 'lizard brain' has run amok and outmanoeuvred the cerebral cortex, carrying out all of the self-destructive behaviours that it loves. In Freudian terms, the id is dominating the ego and superego, driving impulsive and self-destructive behaviour with no regard for consequences or morality.

However, there is a problem with this theory. A few years ago, I searched various psychology, therapy and science sites but could find no general consensus as to which of the three brain sections housed the amygdala. Some say the amygdala is part of the lizard brain, while others say it is located within the mammalian brain. If the amygdala is considered essential in the recognition of danger, how can it not be located in the lizard brain and if it isn't, how do reptiles detect danger?

Following further searching, the reasons for these anomalies in the triune brain theory became clearer.

1. Numerous studies have found that reptiles do have regions of the brain that operate in the same way as the amygdala and that they are capable of emotional learning and feeling emotion (IntechOpen, 2024). This undermines the understanding that it is the lizard part of the human brain,

devoid of emotion, that is responsible for behaviour thought to be unreasonable.

2. Neuroscientist Dr Lisa Feldman Barrett, in *How Emotions are Made* (2017), cited a meta-analysis of data from all published neuroimaging studies on emotions over a 20-year period. When participants were experiencing fear, only 25% showed amygdala activity.

3. Furthermore, Barrett's meta-analysis showed that the amygdala was activated by a variety of situations, such as when learning new information, perceiving pain and meeting new people.

Steffen et al. (2022) argue that an adaptive model of the brain is more accurate than the triune model. They believe that all vertebrates share the same basic brain regions; what varies between them is the size and complexity of these areas. They see emotion and cognition as being inextricably linked and working interdependently. Along similar lines, Barrett (2017) also supports an adaptive model of the brain, emphasizing the brain's ability to use both interoceptive (internal) and exteroceptive (external) information to predict future events and prepare accordingly. Both Steffen et al. and Barrett provide evidence of the limbic and cortical systems working together to adjust brain networks as new information unfolds.

According to how your brain interprets these signals, it will determine whether you have a pleasant or unpleasant feeling. Your perception of this feeling will determine your ensuing emotion (Barrett, 2017). What is crucial here is that the brain uses this information in tandem with data from past experiences to predict what is likely to happen next and create a relevant simulation. If you are anxious, you will be continually predicting threats from the outside world that are incorrect. Simultaneously, your anxiety will be leading you to misinterpret information derived via interoception so that any changes in heartbeat or how hot or cool you feel, for example, will also lead to predictions of threat. As you become increasingly worn down by these prediction errors, it becomes more difficult to distinguish what is actually going on in your world from that which you fear to be occurring.

This might sound very familiar to you. From my own experience of anxiety and from working with anxious clients, exhaustion is universal. When the body constantly prepares for threats that never arrive, and is forced to keep readjusting, it drains your life force—without you having even done anything. Many people with anxiety find themselves needing to sleep immediately after work, school, or social events, simply because they're so worn out.

So, if you have anxiety, how might knowing about this theory help you in any way? Firstly, knowing that how you feel is determined by your brain's interpretation of what is going on in your body is a very good starting point. This means that how you feel is determined by your perception of internal events, not by what is going on in the outside world. This is good news because if it is your perception, then, as seen in the previous chapter, you can change your perception. It is malleable and only you are in charge of it.

This is how I often explain anxiety in sessions. It's a bit like driving a car while focusing on the interior instead of the road ahead. You need to trust that the car is functioning properly until it isn't, and focus your attention on the traffic and where you are going. Similarly, the body is an incredible creation, capable of regulating breathing, digestion, body temperature, and heartbeat. You don't need to be checking in on it every second; your subconscious mind takes care of that beautifully. Your conscious mind is meant for choosing what needs to be done and taking action. The subconscious is brilliantly designed to keep your body running at its best. You need to trust it and stop interfering.

If you have experienced anxiety, you will know that your interprets most changes in the body as a negative event. Ra heart, sweaty palms, a tightness in the chest or shortness of breath are enough for the anxious person to be convinced that a threat is imminent. Unfortunately, at this stage, you will also be tracking the data bank of all your past experiences to find a match for what dreadful thing might be about to happen (but more than likely never will). If you have experienced trauma in the past, you will have a wealth of negative memories to choose from. It doesn't even need to be anything related to what is going on in the present. Your anxiety isn't fussy.

This is the important point. Each person has different information to draw on according to their individual experience; therefore, the emotions you feel will be coloured according to your experience. Furthermore, all it takes is a thought to start the whole process. There doesn't need to be anything going on outside of you. For example, you might have the thought that you haven't finished that project. That leads to you feeling worried that you may not finish it by the deadline. The feeling is familiar, and you immediately begin to track your memory bank for similar examples of not having achieved what you set out to do. Now you really have something to worry about, and creeping dread permeates your whole being. You don't want to talk to anyone and retreat to your bedroom to be able to panic alone. *This entire story has been constructed on the back of one thought.*

So, what can you do about any of this? Can you stop feeling anxious? If you want to get a handle on your anxiety, it can be helpful, first of all, to get an idea of the bigger picture. If you have been believing your anxiety, you are listening to an adaptation that probably developed when you were a child. It is much younger than you and could do with you looking after it, not the other way around. It developed initially as a means of protecting you and would have been appropriate for the situation at the time. A child growing up in an unsafe household, for example, would need to be hyper-vigilant, as an abusive parent might explode at any moment for no apparent reason. However, the rest of the world is not an abusive parent, and hyper-vigilance is costly in terms of the energy expended for little or no return. It is time to recognise who is in charge—you are the boss, not the anxiety.

Any forms of therapy that acknowledge adaptations as having developed initially for the good of the person are helpful. Internal Family Systems (IFS) is a method devised by Richard Schwartz and is very useful because it involves working with the many parts that we all have. He stresses in his book *No Bad Parts* (2021) that all of these parts, however destructive, mean well. The anxious part developed to manage perceived or real danger. A depressed part might have been a response to being unpopular at school or unloved at home. A drinking part might have started as a means of managing shyness, and so it goes on for all of us. The IFS therapist helps the client see that all these parts are trying to help, however misguided they might be. Schwartz recommends not giving them names or characters but helps the client see that each part is them.

However, I have found that for some clients, describing their parts as animals works really well. Clients often say that they hate their anxiety because it ruins everything they try to do. Seeing the anxiety as an animal can help the client find empathy for it more quickly, and once that happens, everything can change. For instance, someone with Borderline Personality Disorder saw their rage as a crow swooping down and attacking in order to protect them. Prior to this development, they had felt shame about their rage, but as they felt empathy and acceptance for the crow, it began to happen less.

Most recently, I have been describing anxiety to some clients as an octopus. You have a negative thought, and your stomach drops. Your chest tightens, and you feel short of breath. The octopus had been sitting at rest. It opens its eyes and then sweeps out from under the rock. It is hunting, and it is fast. One tentacle reaches out, attaches to a subject and draws it in close. It is not letting go and tracks the memory bank for any disaster that could relate to this issue. Oh, wait, the octopus is relinquishing its grip. This is great, but oh no, it is only doing so because one of its other tentacles has found something else to hook on to. Wait, this can't be happening. It's found something else. How can you worry about all of this at once? *Don't speak to me. I'm too busy worrying. I haven't got time to talk. No, I'm not moody!*

So, how can you handle this? Can you fight the octopus so that it goes away? It hasn't worked in the past—it just got stronger when you tried to get rid of it. Anyway, you don't want it to escape because it is all you have to protect you. Ah, I see—you had thought you wanted to get rid of it, but now you are clinging on to it. **You don't think you would survive without it.** After all, who would be checking the environment for danger then? You think that it's all you have to keep you safe. Is there any way it could work with you instead of against you?

You can see that it thinks it is helping and that it is actually rather childlike. It keeps rushing ahead of the game before it even knows what is actually going on. Could you soothe it somehow and ask it to give you a moment? Can you say that you can help look after it, that it doesn't need to be quite so worried and that you have a safe space for it to rest? It seems to be responding well to that. It likes the idea of a rock to hide under. You can see now that it is actually much smaller than you and that it is the one who is afraid. It needs you to help it, not the other way around. You can do that. You have empathy, and you don't want it to suffer anymore. You can take care of it when it rushes out of the rock again. You are feeling much better now.

This idea that the anxiety is younger than you is really important and comes up in multiple theories of anxiety. Professor Steve Peters (2012), in *The Chimp Paradox* refers to it as c. three years of age. When doing Inner Child work, fears are seen to originate from our child self within, so if we work out what the child is remembering from the past that is holding us back in the present, we are able to move forward. In IFS therapy, all the parts are younger than the Self, formed at and frozen in different stages of our development, playing out what might have helped at that stage.

If you can begin to understand that you are in charge, not the anxiety, you will be able to manage it well, rather than it manage you badly. Many people describe waking in the night and ruminating on multiple fears, often regarding family members or partners. If you are worrying about someone, it bears zero benefit to them and cuts you like a knife. Turn this night-time activity on its head. If you wake and begin to imagine your loved one having a car crash or being attacked, know that the recipient would certainly not welcome this and that it is never helpful. Instead, imagine them looking really happy or having arrived where they were travelling. Send them warm, loving feelings and each time you feel the pull towards the drug of worry, turn away from it and send more love. This is reparative for you and the other. Make yourself, rather than your anxiety, the director of what you are imagining.

Moving forward occurs through taking responsibility for the Self in the present day and beginning to realise that your anxiety is not capable of running the show. It is in need of comfort, by you. There is an even bigger picture with regard to anxiety, which can work for some people. It is to know that you will deal with whatever happens because you have dealt with challenges before, and you will deal with them again. It is your choice ultimately whether you go forward with this attitude or of one that says you won't be able to cope. Once you embrace the 'will be able to cope' way of living, your life will improve considerably. You will be unfazed by the challenges ahead. The *Jaws* crew never got their 'bigger boat', but you just did.

Chapter 4

I Can't Help What I Think. Right?

If we return to our theme of taking responsibility for our lives in every moment, then are we responsible for what we are thinking? Most people believe that because their lives are stressful now, negative thoughts are inevitable. They assume that when their situation changes for the better, their thoughts will become positive. However, as Indian guru Sadghuru (2021) says in his book *Karma*, never in the world have we had so much convenience, so why are such a high percentage of so many populations reliant on medication to boost their mood?

Nancy Colier, in her book *Can't Stop Thinking*, cites findings that of the 60,000 – 80,000 thoughts per day humans have, 80% are negative. Production is incessant and whilst we assume we are choosing what we think, this is a misconception. The deluge of thoughts that pass through our minds each day are uninvited. They emerge randomly from the vast content of our subconscious minds, containing any mix of sensory information, facts, emotions and subjective information.

Eckhart Tolle (2011) describes thought forms as though sparks of energy floating around in the collective mind. According to what is going on within us, related thoughts will be attracted to our field of awareness. Consequently, if I am feeling angry, I will be a magnet for angry thoughts. Whilst I think that it is personal, my identification with and experiencing of this anger also affects the collective mind. As I have more experiences that I don't like, I will collect more negative thoughts and the mind I experience as mine becomes increasingly trapped in a spiral of negativity.

Dr Rick Hanson (2020) describes our minds as being like 'Teflon' for positive experiences and 'Velcro' for the negative. This means that unless you understand what is going on, you could very easily slide into a trap of perpetual negative thinking. As you mainly remember unpleasant experiences, this affects your mood, which in turn attracts more negative thoughts and feelings. We aren't talking here about any particular mental health issue. This is the malaise of the masses.

Whilst it might seem concerning to find out that you don't choose your thoughts, this is actually really good news. If you believed you were a bad person because you had horrible thoughts, well, now you have the chance to change your perception of yourself. Yes, your mind is racing with all kinds of ghastly thoughts all day, but you didn't choose them, so maybe you are not these thoughts. If you are not your thoughts, there is some separation between you and them. This is great. This negative junk isn't inextricably interwoven into your very being. It is transient and needn't stick. Maybe, then, if it is not actually you, you can choose the extent to which you engage with it.

I found an explanation given by the American spiritual teacher Ram Dass (Ram Dass & Gorman, 1985) really helpful regarding this subject. He gave the analogy of the mind as a blue sky and dark thoughts as black clouds. He said that when in a low mood, pulling back into awareness the wider picture of the encompassing blue sky can be a reminder that all moods are transitory. He also described receiving a late-night phone call from someone who described himself as having gone completely mad. Ram Dass asked if he could speak to the part of the caller who had been able to dial his telephone number, reminding him that he was still functioning. The man calmed down.

Eckhart Tolle (2024) also explores how to separate yourself from your thoughts, describing the accumulation of old memories, hurts, grievances, and pain as the *pain body*. You might be having a calm conversation with someone and notice them briefly look away. Rather than staying present and attributing their lapse in eye contact to a momentary distraction, the pain body gets activated. Suddenly, you identify as "poor ignored me," begin resenting the other person, and oscillate between self-loathing and self-defence. Once the pain body is allowed in, the effects of that fleeting moment can linger for days. Not only are you replaying your own past grievances, but you are also tapping into similar energies from the collective consciousness. By feeding into it, you are fattening up your pain body and letting it run your life. However, once you become aware of it as a concept, you can create some distance between yourself and it, so that it hijacks you less often. You can put it on a diet.

These examples demonstrate the extent to which we can calm ourselves if we just create a little separation between our thoughts and ourselves. Reading this won't make any difference to you. However, trying it might. I will now give an example of a thinking problem that affects many people and then describe how you might alleviate its effects.

If you are critical of yourself after social interactions, you are likely to keep replaying them in your mind. The scenario might go like this: you had a long conversation with someone and thought they didn't get one of the jokes you made. You tried to shrug it off at the time, maybe drinking more than usual to try to forget. But when you got home, the rot set in. You now produced, wrote the script, starred in, and directed the B movie of that exchange. You can see it all so clearly: you thinking you were being really funny; the other person looking confused and others looking on with disdain. Now that you've made the movie, you can torture yourself indefinitely, rewinding it and playing it back over and over and over again. What joy!

I haven't come across anyone who I have described this to who hasn't identified with it. Thankfully, there is something to be done about it. However, once again, unless you take full responsibility for all you have done to create it and really make the effort to stop it, it will be a waste of your time even reading this.

Prescription for lessening self-flagellation following social interactions:

1. Own the fact that only you have access to this dreadful movie, created by and starring you.

2. Know that you are not responsible for how the other perceived what you said or did.

3. Know that you think you are capable of reading the other's mind and that is not likely unless you have trained yourself to actually do that.

4. Know that most people only care about what they said and did at the party and they will not be spending all week worrying about what you said and did.

5. Rejoice in the fact that only you own the rights to this movie.

6. Know that you can choose how many times to watch this dreadful garbage.

7. Choose how many times you are going to watch it and only watch it that many times. It will become very boring anyway. If it doesn't, you are self-obsessed and need to check yourself.

8. Take full responsibility for your actions on the evening in question and ask yourself if it brought with it any useful learning.

9. Let it go. Watch the movie as many times as you have decided you are allowed to, and then dump it.

10. Any future times you are tempted to go there, just make it a comedy. I imagine a cartoon version of myself chasing myself with a stick, wanting to start up the self-flagellation again. I outrun myself and laugh. That takes about 0.5 seconds.

You might be thinking, *But, what if I did actually do something bad that evening?* Well, if you think you did and take full responsibility for it, you might apologise. However, sometimes, we return to the scene of the crime to soothe ourselves, even if it is of no use to the other. Be honest with yourself. Is there any benefit to the other in your contacting them to apologise? If not, decide what to do with it now:

Prescription for if I think I have been rude, noisy, difficult, boring, outrageous or some other less than perfect behaviour:

1. Is there any benefit to the other for me to apologise?

2. If not, that means I am going to be sitting with this.

3. If I sit with it, I have two choices.

a) Put myself in the guilt prison. This is a very popular choice. How long shall I give myself for the misdemeanour? I know—I will leave it open-ended and torture myself with this one for the rest of my life! Every time I am feeling low, I can wheel out the movie again to make sure I really deserve to feel low.

b) I choose not to put myself in the guilt prison. Instead, I have learned that doing cartwheels at a dinner party doesn't make me feel good afterwards. I will endeavour to avoid that happening again, and then I won't feel I need the guilt prison in future. I take full responsibility for my actions the other night, and I have learned from them. I can still have a good relationship with myself. I forgive myself, and I can actually laugh about this.

4. I have chosen not to put myself in the guilt prison and know that instead I am a good learner. I know guilt keeps me stuck and prevents learning and I am not choosing it. It drags me backwards and encourages negative thoughts. I let it go.

What we have looked at here are some ways of creating space between your thoughts and yourself. That distance can be incredibly helpful, but are there other things you can do to slow down the constant stream of negative thoughts running through your mind? You might want to consider that the information you're currently downloading into your subconscious becomes part of the database from which future thoughts arise. If you want your thinking to be less negative, it might be time to take a closer look at what you are feeding your mind.

Aldous Huxley (BBC Archive, 1961) warned as long ago as the 1950s of the dangers of burgeoning and overcrowded populations being fed managed information via multiple media. George Orwell wrote *1984* in 1939, warning of the manipulation and control of the masses using the media and technology. Here we are in the information era, plugged into phones, tablets, laptops, radios, televisions, newspapers and so the list goes on. How many have taken heed of these warnings? What does it take to wake people up and out of this torpor?

I confess to having been sleepwalking, drone-like, for most of my life, with the occasional moment of wakefulness. However, now that I am awake to the fact that our subconscious mind forgets nothing, I am a lot choosier about what I am plugged into. I am also upfront about it with clients. Where relevant, I will let clients know that the money they are spending on coming to therapy with me is being wasted if they continue to listen to content that fills their minds with negative thoughts.

It's time to do a clean-up. What are you subjecting your subconscious mind to?

Prescription for cleaning up what you are downloading to your subconscious mind:

1. I may not choose my thoughts, but I am responsible for what I am downloading to my subconscious mind. If I want to minimise negative content arising in my conscious awareness, I can choose not to download such content.

2. If I hang out with negative people who complain about how awful the world is, I can change who I hang out with.

3. If I suffer from FOMO, it would not be wise to look at social media.

4. If I think the world is unsafe and get upset by news stories, I will have a break from all news providers and see if that helps.

5. If I doom-scroll, I will give myself a rest from it.

6. I will not read newspapers or listen to any news close to my bedtime. The subconscious is at its most receptive just before and during sleep.

7. I am scared people will think I'm stupid if I don't know what is going on in the news. However, other people regurgitate their news fixes all day long, so I will know what is going on anyway. However, I won't encourage long, bad-news-splurging conversations.

Here, we have looked firstly at some ways to create some distance between your thoughts and yourself, and secondly at ways that might help you reduce the deluge of negative information you are receiving on a daily basis.

Next, we are going to look at what can happen if you don't take responsibility for both how you feel and what you think about. We are going to investigate what could happen to you if you are not in control of these crucial aspects of your life. You may have thought that this is just a personal issue and that it is doing no harm. However, if you aren't in charge of your mind, someone will be. In the next chapters, we are going to investigate why narcissism is becoming such a burgeoning problem and how it might relate to these questions.

Chapter 5

Narcissism - The What and The Why

I have found in the last few years that the main reason for anyone accessing therapy is related in some way to narcissistic abuse. The person may or may not know that is what they are up against, but it usually becomes apparent in the initial consultation or in the first full session. It could be called 'spot the narcissist'—is it the employer, the parent/s, partner, son-in-law, daughter, sister, teacher, colleague or best friend? Unfortunately, for some clients, it may be all of the aforementioned. We will look at why this happens in the next chapter. Many books are written as though all narcissists are men. This is not the case, and there seem to be as many men presenting for therapy to deal with a narcissistic female partner as there are women affected by men. It is also an issue affecting many lesbian, gay, bisexual and transgender couples.

In my work, I name it as soon as I recognise it because if I don't, the client will spend all their energy trying harder to please the narcissist to absolutely zero avail. I also name it because I don't believe it is ethical to take a client's money week after week whilst they try to improve a relationship with someone who has neither the will nor the ability to relate in a fair or healthy manner.

For a long time, many counsellors were in denial of narcissism. I saw a lot of clients who had been in individual or couples' counselling, where the therapist had not recognised that they were dealing with a narcissist. Some therapy sites have articles suggesting that the term is bandied around too easily now and that just because someone is very confident, has high self-esteem and becomes unpleasant during a break-up, it doesn't mean they are narcissistic. This may be the rhetoric on social media, but I haven't experienced it with clients. Most clients have exhausted all other possibilities, and themselves, before they come to the realisation that they are dealing with a narcissist.

What clients are describing is a lot more than high self-esteem and being unkind in a break-up. Some of the problems described are: lack of empathy; lying; self-aggrandisement; jokes at others' expense; superiority; belief in others' inferiority unless they are rich or famous; anger; selfishness; sex/porn/alcohol/drug abuse or addiction; verbal abuse; physical abuse; disregard for the feelings of others; inability to cope with others having an opinion; need to control; victim-mongering; self-pity; name-calling; needing to have an enemy; meanness; inability to recognise partner's career or success; draining of finances of everyone around them; put-downs; resenting others' success; lack of joy and so the list goes on.

This list is not exhaustive, and depending on the kind of narcissist, the cocktail of these traits will vary. This is why it can be so difficult for people to spot narcissism. Narcissism expert Dr Ramani Durvusula (2024) describes six main types. Although there are countless other subtypes, this gives a good overview of what to look out for. You will have encountered some of these or heard other people talking about them:

1. Grandiose narcissist: You may have encountered or had a relationship with a grandiose narcissist, male or female, who was the flashy show-off in public and controlling rager behind closed doors.

2. Coming out of a relationship with a grandiose narcissist makes you perfect fodder for vulnerable narcissists. They will listen to your horror stories regarding the grandiose narcissist and tell you they, too, have suffered in such awful ways. They will say all their exes were 'psychos', just like your ex. They will proclaim that you are soulmates. Once you are hooked, they will start attacking you with the information you gave them about your past. I always know a client is dating a vulnerable narcissist when they say that their friends say that their partner is 'punching above their weight'. The vulnerable narcissist's strategy is to sidle up to someone out of their league, offering themselves as a shoulder to cry on. Once the other becomes reliant on them, the campaign to destroy their confidence begins. By the time the recipient presents for therapy, they will have lost all perspective and their grip on reality. Helpful advice when dating: don't talk about previous abusers. It isn't a badge of honour, and it will attract fresh

abusers like flies around dung. To them, it is confirmation that you can be controlled because you have been before.

3. More confusing is the communal narcissist. You might find this do-gooder: heading up a charity or voluntary organisation; working as a head teacher; acting like a perfect mother; part of or running a spiritual organisation; working as a counsellor or social worker. This kind of work is done to show the world what a good person the narcissist is. The raging, shaming and control will manifest behind closed doors with family and staff. Communal narcissists think they are much nicer than those close to them do.

4. The neglectful narcissist makes an awful partner or parent. They are disinterested in the lives of their families and are rude and dismissive.

5. The self-righteous narcissist is highly judgmental, convinced of their moral superiority and unwavering belief that they are always right. Spiritual communities, unfortunately, are often infested with this type.

6. The malignant narcissist shares many traits with the psychopath and sociopath, including a lack of empathy, a tendency to manipulate others, and aggressive behaviour. Unfortunately, they derive pleasure from harming or controlling people. Clients have described before having been abused on the first date but somehow being manipulated into continuing into a relationship.

One question that clients often ask is why there seem to be so many narcissists nowadays. The general consensus seems to be that, whilst it is highly heritable, certain conditions are more likely to flick that switch on. Some of the common factors are parents overvaluing the child, thus creating a sense of entitlement; parents being overcritical; trauma, such as death of a parent or neglect; parents being intrusive and controlling.

You may feel this is parent-blaming, but parents are born of cultures and eras. In his book *Karma*, Sadghuru (2021) discusses how upset people get if they feel they are being blamed for the difficulties in their children's lives. However, his explanation is a more helpful way of understanding this issue. He describes how karma relates more to memory and action than reward and punishment. One's karma is derived from a number of influences, including the society within which one lives. If our culture places value on unhealthy attributes in our children and we fail to help them develop other, more grounded ways of being, they will adapt accordingly. It is evolution. This isn't just played out at home for the child but in school and with friends. It is reconfirmed in television programmes and on social media. We are providing all the conditions societally for narcissism to propagate. We will look at this further in a later chapter.

I am working in the UK, and I work with clients with narcissistic parents from the UK, Eastern Europe, The US, India, Russia, Germany .... This is a global problem. Whilst COVID-19 was recognised as a pandemic, this is a more insidious and pervasive one. It is a silent spreader, and it is time to recognise it. Most people are in denial of it and enable the behaviour. Employers don't recognise it and often support the narcissist because they are such convincing liars. When someone leaves a narcissistic partner, they also leave behind most of their friends because the friends believe the narcissist. In friendship groups, it is the one who has been picked on who has to move on. When a sibling calls out the behaviour of the narcissistic sibling to parents, the family rallies around the narcissist, pushing out the whistle-blower.

Having said that this is not a case of parent-blaming and the problem is a global one, this does not absolve one single individual from taking responsibility for themselves in this situation. If you haven't been affected by a narcissist as yet, you may think I am exaggerating. If you have, you will know just how awful the effects are. When people present for therapy, whatever the context of the abuse, they will start by saying that they don't know who they are anymore. They will say that they used to be confident, that they don't enjoy anything anymore and wonder why they now have anxiety and depression. Unfortunately, all this is invariably made worse by the enablers, who make excuses for the narcissist's behaviour. They might say: he's just a strong character (bully); she doesn't mean it; he had a difficult childhood; but he's so charming; but she runs a charity, but she's a therapist; he does so much for the community....

You may now be starting to see that narcissism has become commonplace, and if you're on the receiving end, support is likely to be scarce. I hope that by writing this, I can help you see there are ways to recognise it and protect yourself, even if no one believes you. If we go back to the message running throughout this book, the only way you are going to be able to protect yourself is by taking responsibility for yourself.

So, if we are looking at taking responsibility for ourselves in this, it will be helpful to look a little more closely at the conditioning that might lead someone to become a narcissist or their prey. If you are going to take responsibility, you need to understand how it happened to you. In Chapter 2, we looked at how confusion regarding the kind of parenting we receive will lead to deleterious effects in adulthood. Nowhere is the effect of this more obvious than in the way that we relate to others. The extent to which we are aware of this and able to recognise and act on it will determine whether we are driven to exert power over others, give away our power to others or remain secure in our own power.

Patricia Evans (1992) describes how this might occur in 'The Verbally Abusive Relationship'. Evans explains that if a person has no sense of power within them, their only means of gaining one will be by controlling others. This is played out on a macro level with the anthropocentric view that humans have the right to control everything on the planet for their own benefit. It is played out on the micro level in relationships, with one party feeling entitled to control the other. In contrast, those who have a sense of empowerment from within are able to more easily collaborate with others.

This is similar to Sadghuru's (2021) explanation regarding how a child is moulded not only according to what is going on within the family but more widely according to a society's model of the world. If a child grows up in a household where power is exerted over them and comes to accept that model, it aligns perfectly with a worldview in which people hold power over one another and everything else. Both the controller and the controlled have grown up in this environment, but only the controller internalises and repeats the model, believing they are entitled to exert power over others. The controlled, in contrast, sense something was wrong in childhood but continue to idealise the parent — the "great denial" described by Alice Miller (1987). Unable to acknowledge the parent's failings, the child assumes the blame, concluding that they themselves were the problem. This internalised belief strips them of self-esteem and leaves them unprotected in adulthood, unable to recognise or respond to abuse. If people are unpleasant, they believe that they must try harder and any warning signs of abuse are ignored.

For those who internalise the "power over" model and go on to control others, this tendency often develops along two main paths. Those with Narcissistic Personality Disorder (NPD) exert power through dominance, entitlement, and inflated self-importance (Kernberg, 1975). In contrast, individuals who develop Obsessive-Compulsive Personality Disorder (OCPD) seek stability via an excessive need for order, control, and perfectionism (Cain et al., 2015). While both involve controlling others, they do so in very different ways—one through superiority, the other through structure.

No adaptation occurs without good reason at the time, but every adaptation carries a cost. For those who go on to exert power over others, emotional disconnection functions as a defence against childhood despair. Individuals with Narcissistic Personality Disorder (NPD) lack object constancy—the ability to maintain a stable sense of self and of others during conflict or disappointment (Kernberg, 1975). This means that when someone pleases them, that person is seen as entirely good, but when that same person displeases them, they are viewed as entirely bad. It isn't possible, in their view, to be a good person who disagrees with them. While this defence may shield them from emotional pain, it blocks the ability to feel joy or to form genuine connections. Without access to their emotional compass, they struggle to navigate relationships and life in a responsive, dynamic way. Controlling others becomes their only remaining route to feeling any sense of power (Evans, 1992).

The controllable are able to feel, but they have learned to prioritize others' needs over their own. You may not have been in an abusive relationship yourself, but may have witnessed someone appeasing a controlling partner. Fawning is a lesser-known trauma response than fight, flight or freeze, yet for a child with a volatile parent, it would have been essential to avert the next tirade. The fawning that kept them safe in childhood unfortunately becomes maladaptive in adulthood.

Chronic appeasers are more likely to end up in abusive relationships, and this pattern causes them to people-please and approval-seek in every area of life. For those who haven't experienced it, the fear behind these behaviours is hard to explain. It runs deeper than wanting to be liked. It is a creeping dread that something terrible will happen if someone else is displeased. That fear dates back to a time when the child had no power and upsetting a parent carried real danger and/or the withdrawal of love. It is these buried feelings that continue to influence present-day behaviours and they need to be addressed.

Is there anything that can be done to prevent these two trajectories? Sometimes, an adult such as a teacher, counsellor, relation or family friend can demonstrate to the child that there is another way of living and being. This can be enough for that child to realise that they do not have to accept a limited life of control and misery. It will still be the case that they will need to work on the effects of their childhood, but it is made easier if it is clear that it was not a healthy one.

On all of the forums for victims of narcissistic abuse, the focus is on what the narcissist did next, with people comparing notes. However, the behaviours are all the same to a greater or lesser degree and people can get very stuck in this stage. If you have been in this kind of relationship or had this kind of encounter with a colleague or client, it is more important to ask what it is about you that led you to get into this situation. This isn't about wallowing in self-blame but about taking responsibility for your part in it. As discussed in Chapter 3 regarding trauma, unless you can see how you got into something, it is unlikely you will be able to side-step it when it comes your way once more.

In the next chapter, we will look at what makes someone attractive to narcissists. If this is happening to you, you will find that they appear in every aspect of your life so that it begins to seem as though everyone is a narcissist. We will look at why this might be happening and what you can do to avert it.

Chapter 6

Why Am I a Magnet for Narcissists?

This chapter is going to be relevant to you whether you are magnetic to narcissists or not. If you are, then it will help you develop immunity. If you are not, it will help you understand why this is such a prevalent issue and why it matters if you are an enabler of the behaviours. We have looked in the previous chapter at how childhood experience can lead us to become controlling, controlled or self-led. We saw how if a child comes to understand that love is conditional upon how we behave and what we achieve, that develops into people-pleasing behaviours. The people-pleaser has learned to put aside their feelings and put others first, to their own detriment.

In the early 1900s, James Horton Cooley's Looking Glass Self-theory (Simply Psychology, 2023) described how children come to know themselves and develop their identity according to how they perceive others to perceive them. If the child is surrounded by emotionally available adults, that perception will be generally positive and open to fluctuation. For instance, *Mum loves me but she doesn't like it when I hit my brother. I'm known as a hard worker at school, but I don't enjoy sports.*

In this way, the child who is developing in a healthy way comes to understand via others' perception of them a sense of their identity. This child is able to remain connected to their feelings and their emotional compass, so that if something difficult is experienced they are able to discern from their feelings that it is not okay. As they navigate friendships, they will probably be able to tell if someone is being unkind and know that they don't want that.

For the child surrounded by adults who are emotionally unavailable, development will be distinctly different. If the parents are critical and dismissive, the child might express sadness and be told that there are people far worse off and to get over it. If the child is excited, they might be told to shut up and stop being annoying. If the child is hit, they might be told not to cry because they deserved it.

Over time, they lose the ability to trust the meaning of their feelings. Feelings act as a compass. If we are in tune with them, when they arise from our subconscious and are experienced in our bodies, they will signal what action we might need to take, if any. The child primed to mistrust their feelings has had their ability to skilfully navigate relationships and life impaired.

This pressure to disregard one's own feelings also occurs when parents place high standards on their children. These children are taught that love is conditional upon high grades and good behaviour. The child might prefer to study art rather than physics but is told that art won't help them get into the top universities. The parents might be dismissive of people they feel are of lesser intelligence than they are. The child is likely to develop into an adult with a fear of seemingly intelligent adults in authority. The child will seek perfectionism, pushing down all feelings in its pursuit. For the perfectionist adult, even the smallest mistakes are intolerable.

This is what we looked at in the last chapter. Unable to recognise what they feel from within their own bodies, these children will start to search for that information in the external environment. With the loss of their own emotional compass, they lose the ability to listen to and decipher any feeling, good or bad. They no longer trust how they feel. They don't enjoy parties, but Dad said normal children do enjoy parties, so they make themself dance whilst crying inside. The adults in their lives have trained them to believe that others can tell what they are feeling better than they are able to. They no longer know what they like or what they feel. They have been trained to hand over their remote control to any passer-by who will take it.

So, this child is now on a set of wheels and has a remote control that can direct them wherever a controller wants. They have been programmed to defer to the other. If someone else seems to know what is going on, they will be deferred to. The stage is perfectly set for a controller. Enter the narcissist, stage left. Just like the Wizard of Oz, they have the smoke and mirrors to make themselves seem magnificent and able to fix any problem. Behind all the razzmatazz resides a self-loathing and cringing Gollum.

The tragedy for narcissists is that unless they believe that people see them as magnificent, the charade cannot be maintained, risking a collapse into self-loathing. This is a high-maintenance adaptation. This is why I say that if you go into a relationship with a narcissist, repent at leisure. You are trapped because the supply you are giving them is what they believe they need to stay afloat; it is their life force. You disappear and the illusion of their superiority vanishes, leaving in its place emptiness and despair. That is why the term narcissist is interchangeable with energy vampire or emotional vampire. They will feed off your energy until you are reduced to a shell of your former self and then attack you for being so weak.

You may be wondering how this relates to a vulnerable narcissist because they don't present in this grandiose way. They are self-pitying and more prone to victim-mongering. However, this is deceptive because whilst this might present on the top layer, just beneath is as intense a craving for admiration and power as felt by the grandiose narcissist. Vulnerable narcissists resent most successful people, believing that if they weren't so unlucky, the world would realise they, too, are geniuses. The next Van Gogh or Bob Dylan. It's just not fair that they haven't yet been discovered.

However, what nearly all narcissists have in common is that they will make promises in order to connect. This is because they loathe themselves deep down and so feel that they must present something special in order for you to pick them. For the grandiose kind, it is essential to be somebody, so that they will name-drop, talk about how much they earn and generally big themselves up. This is in direct opposition to when someone well-known describes wishing to meet someone who really likes them for who they are, not their fame. The vulnerable narcissist will pretend to be caring and sensitive to attract a partner. They will usually talk about how 'I was almost famous, but I was robbed'.

The controllable meets the controller, and the fit is like the two clasps of a car seat-belt clicking together. It feels perfect for a very short amount of time. The narcissist is getting admiration or sympathy, depending on the type, and the controllable is being looked after by someone who presents as either strong or sensitive. Unfortunately, narcissists are neither strong nor sensitive in any healthy or helpful way. The charade will not last long, but usually long enough for the controllable to be hooked.

If it is in the workplace with a colleague or boss, the compliments that once flowed so freely soon give way to random insults. The narcissist seems confident, and people laugh at their constant jokes. It's worrying to be a disappointment to them. You try harder to get things right, but the attacks are unprovoked and unpredictable. Eventually, you are signed off sick and present for therapy, saying that you used to love your job and can't understand what went wrong. You may still be trying to be liked by the narcissist, because they don't seem to be doing it to anyone else. You feel that if you weren't such an idiot, it wouldn't have happened to you. Other people seem to like them, so you feel isolated and afraid. You are loath to speak out, because you don't feel anyone will believe you. You think it may be your fault anyway, because you never were very confident.

You will all have heard of love-bombing, and in all of these scenarios, the controllable will have succumbed to its magnetic pull. If you don't like yourself, you constantly search for others to like you. This will never be enough because unless you stop the self-dislike, you won't believe them anyway. You will never feel good enough. Love-bombing arrows fall to the ground when aimed at someone who is confident in themselves. Flattery and false adulation are surplus to requirement for someone who already feels good about who they are.

When dealing with clients who have grown up with narcissistic parents or siblings, it is clear they did not play a part in a transaction that led them into the situation. It is important to help the person understand that it was not their fault that they were born into a family containing narcissists. However, I find that in domestic abuse services, when dealing with adult relationships, it is always stressed that it is not the fault of the 'victim' for walking into the relationship. Most people get into these relationships because of the conditioning we have been looking at and, yes, it does take a considerable shift in consciousness to wake up out of this. However, it is far more empowering when those who have experienced abuse are helped to understand what led them into the relationship. This isn't about blaming them, but about giving them back a sense of agency.

When exploring with clients, it is clear that there were always warning signs that were ignored. This is because going into a relationship with a narcissist is transactional on both sides. There is a gain to ignoring the warning signs. The narcissist craves connection but lacks the ability to love. Wanting admiration, they mimic what they believe a good partner should be. In many cases, I believe this is delusion rather than conscious manipulation. They genuinely want to be the perfect partner, just as the other person wants it to be true. By adopting the role of a loving person, they attract someone capable of love—hence the love-bombing: 'Ever since I first saw you… You are my soulmate… I would never hurt you.'

The controllable person is a mix of self-doubt and self-loathing. They are looking for an external source to tell them that they are worth something and for someone who seems to know what is going on. It doesn't take much flattery to hook them and reel them in. If they weren't so desperate to be worth something to someone else, they would have seen through the display from the beginning. Also, due to their own lack of confidence, the false confidence of the narcissist is compelling. The narcissist will be saying, 'I can take care of you…. I'll never let you down…. You don't need to worry any more'.

The narcissist needs to feel superior in order to have any sense of power. Here comes a potential partner who is looking for someone strong and to whom they can hand over the reins. Narcissists will often present as functioning and in charge of their lives. If the partner lacks confidence and looks up to the narcissist, when the put-downs begin, they will believe that they just need to try harder. The narcissist was so nice at the beginning, and they just want to get back to that warm, safe place. It becomes like chasing the dragon, trying anything to get back to that first high. They may get the odd crumb of the love-bombing from the early days, but over time this will dry up to be replaced by contempt.

The responsibility lies as much with each party because they are both looking for someone to make them feel better. If you don't like yourself, why should anyone else like you? You are going to make yourself a nuisance in any relationship until you sort out the most important relationship you will ever have, that with yourself.

Let's return to the title of this chapter. If you are a magnet for narcissists, it is because you are looking for something for nothing from them as much as they are looking for something for nothing from you. You went for the super surge of love-bombing for five minutes of inflated self-worth instead of the slow plod of a healthy relationship. If you would like to develop immunity from narcissists, all you need to do is question why someone would want to *persuade* you to be in a relationship with them. Is this person selling themselves to you, and if so, why?

You may find what I am writing irritating because you don't want to take responsibility for what happened, but I am not saying blame yourself and roll around in time-wasting guilt. I am saying own your part in it so that when a narcissist next attempts to draw you in, you will understand what is going on. No one secure within themselves would make promises of a wonderful relationship when they have just met someone. If you recognise that you chose to believe such vacuous assurances before, you can now decide to treat similar behaviours with healthy scepticism. Then, at the very least, you'll have the power to choose whether to walk into what will be another unhealthy relationship.

I personally am now aware that if someone is trying to persuade me to do something I know I don't want, I feel a knot in my stomach and a push-and-pull sensation as I grapple with them verbally. Manipulators are the only people who evoke this feeling in me, and so I listen to my gut and act on it. If this is happening to you, there is no need to give long explanations, just be clear you mean no. If you give reasons, they are another hook that will be used to reel you in. If you are pushed into agreeing to something you don't want to do, remember that you can always change your mind. You can say that you agreed because you were persuaded, but that you can see on reflection that it wasn't the right choice for you.

People with ADHD are six times more likely than those without to have experienced childhood abuse and to become involved in unhealthy adult relationships (Very Well Mind, 2024). ADHD, like narcissism, is highly heritable and is more likely to be activated following childhood trauma. ADHD and narcissism share some traits, such as impulsivity, low boredom threshold, attention difficulties and interrupting conversations. However, the reasons behind these behaviours differ. For instance, the narcissist feels superior and thinks people want to listen to them speak endlessly about themselves, whereas the person with ADHD misjudges when to enter the conversation.

The difficulties experienced with narcissism relate more to a disorder of the self and relationships, whereas ADHD is a neurodevelopmental disorder. However, those with ADHD also have a negative view of self because of the impact of the condition on everyday functioning. In addition, ADHD is often comorbid with heightened sensitivity in interactions with others and with the environment. Narcissists cannot manage criticism of any kind, and this might seem similar to the sensitivity of the person with ADHD. Unfortunately, narcissists always dodge responsibility for any problems, and those with ADHD often assume it. This is the perfect match for abuse to occur within.

Those with autism are also much more likely to get into abusive relationships than neurotypicals. This is due in part to taking at face value what people say. I have found in my work with autistic clients that whatever the abuser says, they can find a way of seeing that it could be right. Maybe once they said something unkind to somebody and the abuser will remind them of that in each argument so that they feel the abuse is justified. This is also the case for neurotypicals who have been brought up to do as their parents say, not as they do.

In addition to this, where there is neurodivergence in a family, narcissism is close by. Whether a mother, father, sibling, grandmother, aunt, or all of them, it will be there. Therefore, the likelihood for neurodivergent people to get into abusive relationships is further raised. The conditioning will have been there from childhood. Combine this with the difficulties fitting in, rejection sensitivity and approval-seeking that most neurodivergent people experience, and it's easy to see how difficult it would be to recognise a manipulator. The manipulator easily detects these insecurities and makes tempting but empty promises of stability and love to draw in their next target.

I could write a lot more on this, but I feel it is enough for now as I want to move on to what it is like to repent at leisure having entered into a relationship with a narcissist. If you are a magnet for narcissists, they will keep coming past you as if on a conveyor belt. You may have been wasting precious life energy by engaging with each and every one. I want you to get to the wonderful position of being able to let them whizz on by without even having noticed you.

In the next chapter, we are going to look at why it will be beneficial to let them pass by you without any interest. If you are someone who craves love-bombing and doesn't want to give that up for less intense relationships, Chapter 7 is for you. This is similar to helping someone struggling with alcohol stay mindful of the hideousness of the hangover to help prevent a relapse. I want to help you keep in mind all the horrors that you can experience if you get entangled with a narcissist in an intimate relationship. I also want you to understand, if you haven't experienced it, just how awful it will be if you try to raise children with a narcissist.

Chapter 7

Narcissistic Hangover: The Aftermath

The baddies in all cautionary tales would now be recognised as narcissists. Hansel and Gretel's stepmother was definitely one, and their father was an enabler. Likewise, Cinderella's father enabled her to be controlled by the stepmother. Rumpelstiltskin was such a controlling rager, he stamped his foot through the floor—and so the list goes on. However, I feel that some real-life examples will be far more useful.

If you succumb to the love-bombing, you will at first be high on the inflated self-worth. Make the most of it because these five minutes of euphoria are costly. You will pay with months, perhaps years, of the most horrendous comedown you could possibly experience. If you have never been in a relationship with a narcissist, you may feel this list is not relevant to you. It absolutely is. Going back to the previous chapters and the theme running through this book regarding taking responsibility, this list may not be the outcome of your life. However, if you have children, it could be their future if you don't take action to prevent them from being conditioned to defer to the other. Wake up!

If you are starting out in your relationship with a narcissist and have noticed some warning signs but are trying to ignore them, get out now. You might still have a grip on reality. Once the put-downs, dismissing, controlling, raging and ignoring step-up, you will gradually lose your footing. Defending yourself will become increasingly difficult.

If you are struggling financially and think you can handle the narcissistic traits because this man or woman is promising to take care of you, think again. Remember that narcissists think that your money is their money. In time, they will spend everything that you have and then try to extract from those around you. Their initial generosity was a means of reeling you in and will dry up once you are hooked. Once your money has gone, escape will be much more difficult.

If you think you will be okay because you have your career, your confidence in that will soon wane. They are unable to handle a partner's success and will begin to undermine you. They will do this behind closed doors, but to the outside world, they might praise your successes because you are their possession. Your success is their success.

The narcissist is funny, and everyone seems to like their jokes, so you feel you should laugh at the ones that are at your expense. You don't want to seem like you don't have a sense of humour. Sarcasm, jokes at your expense and put-downs are verbal abuse and will only get worse. Whilst physical abuse frequently but not always follows verbal abuse, verbal abuse always precedes physical abuse (Evans, 1992). This is a warning sign—leave now! Your willingness to put up with it is confirmation to the narcissist that you can be controlled and won't complain. You are on wheels. Someone who felt good about themselves would ask why they would want to be with someone who made them feel bad.

You will probably be moved away from friends and family so that you become isolated and even easier to control. This will be done in such a way that it seems to be a good idea.

The control will increase once you agree to live with them, get married or engaged.

The narcissist will usually want children as quickly as possible so that you become vulnerable and less able to escape. It is the easiest shackle to place around your ankle. Like you, the children will be a possession.

If the narcissist is male, the control will increase once you are pregnant. If the narcissist is female, the fact that she is pregnant means your workload will soar. If not already the case, you will be expected to do everything. The pregnancy will be weaponised.

However, if the narcissist is a female vulnerable narcissist, you will be shut out because only they know what the child needs. A female vulnerable narcissist will probably home-school the child because nobody else will be good enough to teach them. She will have fallen out with most of the teachers and will have been affronted by the parents. Home-schooling also gives her the excuse not to work for years so that you will have to work harder. She can also boast about the standard of the child's work as it is for her glory, not their benefit. You won't be able to argue with her because, statistically, your child will probably be autistic and/or have ADHD, and she will say the child is too anxious to go to school. Most of the child's anxiety will actually be learned from and caused by the anxious and controlling mother.

Unfortunately, home-schooling means the child gets no escape from the raging, as school is at least a break from both it and her control.

Male vulnerable narcissists like to be the house husband and do school runs. They never quite manage to get back into the workforce again. They might do a little bit of work on their computer but fall out with most clients. You are their financial supply.

Male and female vulnerable narcissists will have a number of health conditions that give them carte blanche to control. They can blame other family members for causing a 'flare-up' or demand peace and quiet because they are so 'unwell'. Food allergies are very popular because they believe it gives them the right to control everything going on in the kitchen.

If your children are lucky, the narcissist will be able to tolerate them in primary school. However, as soon as they have opinions, the narcissist won't be able to cope.

If there is more than one child, there will be a 'golden child' and a 'scapegoat', and if there are three, there will also be a 'lost child'. Every day will have the same nightmarish quality. You will try to protect the scapegoat from the raging and will be attacked for doing so. The golden and lost child will be encouraged to attack the scapegoat but will also be attacked themselves. They all need your help, but your intervention will never be enough to help any of them sufficiently. You will feel as though you are drowning in quicksand. They will all feel you have let them down, and you will have done because there is no way of successfully managing this.

You will all be hyper-vigilant and will develop some of the following: anxiety, stomach conditions, skin conditions, eating difficulties, depression, OCD, ADHD and PTSD, and unfortunately, some children will develop narcissism. Some will develop Complex PTSD and some BPD. Auto-immune conditions that would probably have lain dormant will be triggered.

You will all be walking on eggshells. However, you may as well throw eggs at him or her because there is nothing you can do to avert the explosions. They are addicted to the raging and get a hit from it. One day, it will be because the dinner is too hot, and the next, because it isn't hot enough.

Abuse occurs in a cycle. You will notice calm for a short period of time and might feel a bit high because it is such a relief. Then you notice their eyes go cold, and although they say they are fine, their voice is mean and unpleasant, and their smile fake. The tension is rising, and the whole household senses it. Then comes the explosion, followed by thrashing about and raging like an oversized toddler (which is the emotional age you are dealing with). They will then go into a passive-aggressive sulk whilst they ride out the adrenaline from the high. Once over, they might be sorry (unless a malignant narcissist), but it is self-pity, not remorse. They might beg for forgiveness and warble on about never doing it again … ra … ra … blah … blah….

This is where the amnesia universally sets in. Nearly all clients forget how bad it is when it goes quiet again.

This is why this list is important, and if you are in this situation, I would like you to write your own list. The amnesia will prevent you from getting out because you will keep saying that it isn't that bad and you can handle it. **It is that bad, and you can't.** Write down every disgusting thing that has been done to you and your children and refer to it every day. Become horribly familiar with it. Imagine showing the list to the children's teacher at school or to a friend. This will help you see it through the eyes of someone who is not in denial.

When they have raged at your children and scared, dehumanised, humiliated and crushed them, you will want to comfort the children. The narcissist will prevent you in any way they can from helping. This is the example I give to younger clients, male or female, who may be considering having a baby with a narcissist. There is nothing more exciting to a narcissist than preventing the other parent from comforting the children. This is the level of sickness you are dealing with. This is how bad it will get. This is torture for a loving parent, and this will probably happen most days.

If you have decided that you want to get out of the relationship, you will be moving into a new chapter of difficulties. The worse a partner is, the more complicated the divorce/separation will be. If you are lucky, the narcissist will meet someone else and disappear. However, usually, they stick around to cause trouble.

This is the most dangerous stage of the relationship. When you cut off the supply, they risk dropping down into narcissistic collapse. Their source of admiration and ability to control is in jeopardy, and they have nothing to lose. *It just isn't fair after all they have done for the family.* If the abuse wasn't already physical, it is much more likely to become so now and the risk of being killed increases. They see themselves as victims and so justify to themselves any vengeful acts. Don't underestimate the danger: let friends or family know you are trying to leave; have a bag ready; contact domestic abuse services; have a safe room; and call the police if needed.

In the couples' therapy book *I Love You, but I'm Not in Love with You,* Andrew G Marshall says that when couples get together, they are at the same level of emotional awareness. This is sobering and shows why you must get therapy. **You came into the relationship as lacking in awareness as a narcissist.** In order to help your children, you are going to need to mature emotionally. They will have experienced countless degrading situations, and they will need substantial help and support.

You may be tempted to get into another relationship. Narcissism expert Dr Ramini Durvusula (2024) recommends waiting at least a year to get yourself in order. I would recommend much longer because the children are going to be shell-shocked and in need of stability. They don't need to go through the instability of you falling in love. You need to keep a clear head.

If you do meet another narcissist, they will be nice to your children to reel you in. Some children are taken in by the apparent kindness. Others sniff out the charade in no time and dare to voice their concern. At this point, the non-narcissistic parent often says to the children, 'Can't you be happy for me?' If you find yourself saying this to your children, this is a warning sign that you are not ready for a relationship. They have had an awful start in life and you want them to be pleased you are bringing another adult into their lives. This makes no sense. You need to create the conditions for repair in their lives, not bring in another potentially abusive adult. In order for your children to ever trust you again, you will need to become trustworthy.

If you do get into another relationship, you need to really study the warning signs of narcissism and be aware of every type because statistics show that you are highly likely to meet another narcissist.

In his book *Spiritual Bypassing*, Robert Augustus Masters (2013) warns that while people assume they are consenting to the intimate relationships they embark upon, this may be misleading. You might think that as an adult, you are sufficiently mature to consent to sex. However, most therapeutic modalities acknowledge that all adults have an inner child who is stuck in the past. If your inner child feels worthless and craves attention, don't let it cajole you into giving consent. If you are seeking a new relationship, remember that only a very young part of you could have been fooled by a narcissist's sales pitch. This part needs care and guidance so that you don't make decisions based on its childlike search for approval. If you do, you will be fooled again. Sit yourself down and ask: 'Am I going into this because I want to feel as though I am worth something?' If so, pause. Be kind to your inner child and remind them that they are enough, and there is no need to do anything to gain worth. Only then will you be able to enter any future relationship adult to adult.

If you hook up with another narcissist, your children will have two abusive adults in their lives. The new narcissist may also have children who are narcissists in the making, and they will have access to your children.

You may feel that you are the 'good' parent, but the reality is that you exposed your children to years with a narcissist and will have enabled the behaviour. French psychologist Alice Miller (1987) said that our children's love is earned, and if you didn't protect them, they may not forgive you or love you. Don't complain. Work hard to become more present, don't bring any fresh narcissists into the family and apologise for the damage you have been complicit in. Don't feel sorry for yourself, and don't wallow in guilt. You are not going to be emotionally available to help your children repair if you do that. They need you to grow, mature, be present and above all demonstrate that you love them and you are sorry. This is the time to start earning their love.

Following the break-up, many children say that the non-narcissistic parent is racked with guilt. They say that they feel unable to talk to them about how they feel because they know the parent blames themselves for not having protected them. The self-imposed guilt prison is very tempting because it implies that although you have done things you are not proud of, you feel bad. This helps you feel that you are a good person, after all; one who is remorseful. However, guilt avoids the taking of responsibility. Far better for the children if you are able to say that you are really sorry that you didn't protect them. Find an age-appropriate way of explaining that abuse is unacceptable and that it was your conditioning and lack of awareness that led you into the situation. Explain that you are now more aware and are making changes so that you can be there for them moving forward. With this honesty and embracing of responsibility as opposed to guilt, you become approachable to your children.

If you couldn't parent in the way that you wanted when you were in the relationship, then learn what is required now. If your children don't have contact with you, prepare yourself for if and when they return so that you can be present and be what they need you to be. Reparent yourself, forgive yourself and be grateful that you have the chance to rebuild your life. You can only benefit from this.

Whether you have lived through this yourself, are a parent, plan to become one, or none of the aforementioned, it is still important to understand the kind of environment that supports healthy child development. One of the most crucial distinctions is between false confidence and a quiet, steady sense of inner self-assurance. Psychologist Dr. Mary Ann Little, in her book *Childhood Narcissism* (2023), explores how certain parenting practices can increase the likelihood of a child developing narcissistic traits. She contrasts these with the kinds of approaches that foster emotional resilience, empathy, and healthy self-esteem—qualities essential for raising well-adjusted children.

It is no surprise that unconditional love tops Little's list of recommendations for parents. She explains that when a child grows up knowing they are lovable just as they are, without needing to earn approval or meet conditions, they develop a solid foundation of self-worth that stays with them for life. Children need to be encouraged to try new things, develop skills, and discover what they enjoy. If they don't succeed at first, it's important they are encouraged to try again. Little emphasises that children need to evaluate how good they are at something, so that false praise is unhelpful. It is more beneficial to praise their effort and improvement than to focus on an end goal. Furthermore, she underscores the need to distinguish between expecting respect and expecting to be treated as superior to others.

This last point is really pertinent. I can recall in the 1990s there being an emphasis placed on telling children they were special. Many of the people then becoming parents had not had this kind of 'new-age' rhetoric when growing up. It was described as a means of building self-esteem within the child. However, it was promoted without sufficient detail or consideration of the perils. When children are told they are special by parents, they go to school expecting special treatment from peers and teachers. What would be much more helpful would be to say to the child, 'You are special to me because I am your mum/dad, and I love you. That doesn't mean that you are special to others. You are just the same as the others, but you are really special to me'. However, it can be stressed that your child is unique because each of us is unique and has something different to offer the world.

What is really interesting about the advice proposed by Little regarding raising a well-balanced child is that it is also what is needed by a partner/parent coming out of an unhealthy relationship. We have looked at the conditioning that is likely to lead an adult into an unhealthy relationship. We have considered that anyone going into such a relationship has a stunted level of emotional awareness. Little's advice is really useful advice for reparenting oneself so that future relationships with narcissists can be avoided and a format for parenting can be applied to self and child. You may find when coming out of a relationship with a narcissist that your children are more mature than many of your own parts. You will need to work hard to bring forward all of those very young parts of you that led you into danger. If you can do that, your life and all relationships will improve.

This chapter is a bitter pill to swallow. It is meant to be. I hope that it has given some insight into the impact of creating a family with a narcissist. I hope that it is influential in helping you to take responsibility for yourself and in teaching your children how to do so as well. The more people who understand where being conditioned to defer to another can end, the more people will say no to these kinds of relationships. It is essential that we stop conditioning our children to think that anyone else is capable of telling them how they feel. We are taking away their ability to use their intuition and protect themselves.

In the next chapter, you may be surprised to find that I am going to give thanks to all narcissists out there. However, this is not to condone or enable their behaviour. All evolutionary changes have unexpected benefits and this is what we are going to look at next.

Chapter 8

Why We Should Be Grateful to All Narcissists

So far in this book, we have looked at why it is beneficial to take responsibility for oneself in life and the perils of failing to do so. We have looked at how our childhood conditioning can lead us into becoming controllable or controlling. This is not a problem for the minority. In the UK, one in four women experience domestic abuse and one in six men. The figures are thought to be much higher than this as so much goes unreported. In my work with young women in the UK, it has become commonplace for them to report being physically hurt during sexual encounters with men.

It is estimated that one in 20 people in the UK and US have Narcissistic Personality Disorder (NPD). However, narcissism is on a spectrum and expert Dr Ramini Durvusula (2024) says that as many as one in six people are narcissists. We have looked at the fact that many of those getting involved in relationships with narcissists are neurodivergent. This is also increasing, with up to 15% of people in the UK diagnosed with ADHD and/or autism and many more undiagnosed. All of the aforementioned are highly heritable. This means that increasing numbers of children will be born with a high likelihood of neurodivergence and/or narcissism. It is not difficult to see that this is a burgeoning issue. This is evolution. We are adapting. There will be increasing numbers of unhealthy relationships affecting increasing numbers of children.

Most people have difficulty recognising the traits of a narcissist and so do get reeled into relationships with them, whether intimate, work-related or friendships. If people haven't experienced narcissistic abuse, it is very difficult to help them see that the horrors listed in the previous chapter will happen. Narcissists can be charming, and people who don't see through the games want to be liked by them.

So, what can be done to curb this tide and what can you do to make a difference? If you have fallen victim to narcissistic manipulation, you are unlikely to have come through unscathed. I often ask clients just how big a jolt they needed to wake up? Was this the relationship that caused them to say 'no more'? If this has happened to you, it is a huge gift from the narcissist. The narcissist may have crushed you just enough for you to realise that it's time to take full responsibility for yourself, in everything you do and in every relationship you enter. Although it may have been incredibly painful, you can work positively with this knowledge and use it to power you forward.

There is a choice regarding how far you go with this process. I describe it as a huge gaping wound on the shoulder. You come out of this situation with the wound, and it can't be ignored. You can just stitch it up and put a bandage over it. It will heal over, but you won't understand how it happened or how to prevent it from happening again. You will probably need a number of coping mechanisms in order to ignore it, such as drinking, overeating, restricting eating, overexercising, vaping, dating apps or taking drugs. It may be pressed down, but it will leak out, affecting all relationships going forward. You won't be able to trust anyone because you won't understand what happened to you last time and the time before that.

Alternatively, you could climb inside the wound and walk around in it, investigating everything about it and yourself. You can find out why you invited the narcissist in to make that wound with you. You will then step through the wound and out the other side to a transformed you. Wound, what wound?

Which would you prefer? For those of you who choose the latter, you are the ones who can be grateful to all the narcissists who have led you to this point. It doesn't matter how far you had to go in order to get there. This is what it took to wake you up. It doesn't have to be in an intimate relationship. It could be a work-place situation that led you to this point. It may have been a friendship or your narcissistic adult child. Once you get it and begin to work on taking full responsibility for yourself so that you will not be controlled by others, you will be grateful to all who led you to this point.

American spiritual teacher Ram Dass (2015) used to describe the difficult people and situations in our lives as our gurus in drag. This is a really helpful approach because it makes it more possible to learn from difficult experiences, rather than let them weigh you down. Boxers might have a powerful punch, but ideally, they are really quick on their feet so that they can dodge the punches of the opponent. The more you allow every hurt to sink in and affect you, the slower your reactions will become. If you treat difficult people and circumstances as learning experiences, you will become as fleet of foot as Muhammad Ali. If you are stuck in the past, complaining about how mean everyone has been, you will become increasingly sluggish in your ability to respond. You will become a sitting duck.

So, you are choosing to be grateful to all those who have led to your waking up. What now? If you have learned that you don't want to be controlled, how do you move forward? This is alien territory for you. A new frontier. It means firstly learning how to say no. If you are a people-pleaser, you will find this really difficult. You will be afraid that people won't like you. You want people to think you are a nice person. However, if we look at this closely, you might change your mind. People-pleasers aren't nice people on the inside.

If this is you, you may feel insulted, but stay with me, and you'll see what I mean. If you feel that you have to do more to stay in any relationship than the other, you will be full of resentment for the other. Initially, as the other seems pleased with the efforts you are making, you like them, but as soon as they don't return the favour or don't seem grateful, the internal complaining begins. *It's not fair. After all, I have done for them. They're just not grateful. I don't see why I should....* It would be more respectful to the other to say no in the first place and not set them up to fail. You would have a much greater chance of having a good relationship with them.

This issue around helping others causes discomfort when discussed. People sometimes believe that I am saying that it is good to be selfish. I explain it like this. For a people-pleaser, helping is compulsive, so it is no longer possible to distinguish between altruistic and selfish acts. I am not saying don't help people, but I am saying don't be dishonest about the reasons.

Similarly, eating is essential. This means that if someone has a tendency for overeating, it can be difficult to determine what food is needed and what is surplus to requirement. For an over-exerciser, exercise is clearly essential, but once it is a compulsion, it is very difficult to determine whether that run is helpful or to feed the compulsion. In all of these areas, it can be necessary to strip back to basics in order to remember how to do the act without it being compulsive.

Making this change will begin to change your view of others. You will begin to see things more clearly. You are not a really lovely person who will do anything for anyone. What you had been doing was purely transactional, but in secret. The other didn't know the deal, and yet you were complaining about them for getting it wrong. Moving forward, you are going to initially replace doing too much for the other by not offering to help with anything. You are going to go cold turkey and not allow yourself to offer unless you have really thought it through on your own in private. You will not let yourself offer to do anything in the moment. You will add a 24-hour delay, and if you still feel after that cooling-off period that you do want to offer, then fine, go ahead. In this way, you will begin to know when you are prepared to help with something. If you are only prepared to do it for something in return, that is fine, but be up front about it. Tell the truth so that the other knows they are making a transaction with you.

As a people-pleaser, you will have been dishing out compliments everywhere. Stop being obsequious and know that you are really doing it in the hope that people will like you or give you a compliment in return. You felt it wasn't fair that you always commented on their nice outfits when they never once mentioned yours. Don't allow yourself to compliment anyone unless you are blown away by something. The other does not need your approval, and you need to learn how not to need theirs. It would be much better to find out if they seek out your company without you flattering them.

This way, you will see that they might actually enjoy spending time with you.

You probably feel that you are responsible for how others feel. If you don't do what they want you to do, they will be upset, and it will be your fault. You don't want to go to the party but assume they won't be able to bear the disappointment, so force yourself to go. When you assume that others will be annoyed or upset, you are mind-reading and probably badly. This is making negative assumptions about how others will react without being sufficiently courteous to ask. Remember, you have struggled to know how you feel, so it is highly unlikely you will get it right regarding others.

Start with your own feelings. Do you want to go to the party? No, you won't know anyone, it is a long way from home, and you have work in the morning. Give a simple reason and let it go. This will be hard at first because you will assume the host will be angry. Allow yourself to feel afraid, but do it anyway and carry on. If this seems too scary, start with something smaller.

If you have been in a relationship with a narcissist, you will be very used to being blamed for having made them angry. You didn't make them angry. They have a lot of anger within them, just below the surface, and there doesn't need to be a reason for it to spill. You may be really fearful of evoking anger in others, but that is their responsibility, not yours. If they do get angry in your presence, it has to do with how they respond to situations, and you may decide you don't want to spend time with friends with anger issues anymore. As you begin to recognise that someone else's anger is their issue, you will be able to take more responsibility for your part in situations. Maybe you did do something regrettable. You can always apologise for your part in it.

You may have a habit of always agreeing with the views of others, both to avoid conflict and to make them like you. When making plans with friends, you probably said you didn't mind what the decision was. You were easy either way. This isn't good for your friends as it places all the responsibility on them. Begin to say what you want to do. If the trip goes wrong, so what? If the people are friends, they'll get over it. You may have pretended to like certain music or activities in order to fit in. Really begin to think about what you do like. This will be difficult if you have always tried to fit in with others.

If you are accustomed to laughing at people's jokes because you feel you should, try stopping it. Endless laughing at dull jokes is tiring and boring. Try an experiment of only laughing when something is actually funny. This way, you won't be encouraging the people around you to engage in wisecracks that aren't funny and that are usually at other people's expense. You will begin to discover what is really funny.

If you do enjoy the company of people who use sarcasm and put-downs, it is probably because in your family of origin it was the norm. In domestic abuse therapy groups, women will often be really disappointed when this subject is discussed. They will say that men who don't joke around are boring and that they are attracted to a good sense of humour. If this is you, this is your conditioning. You have been trained to join in whilst others verbally abuse you. *Don't rock the boat ... don't make a fuss ... be a good girl ...don't make other people uncomfortable by complaining....* It only becomes safe to laugh at yourself once your self-loathing is sorted out. Until that point, you will need to wilfully practise not joining in the attacks on you by others. Sarcasm is the first stage of verbal abuse—avoid it. Ask the person if they feel what they are saying would be acceptable without it being dressed up as a joke.

These suggestions are the starting point for shaking off the conditioning of being controllable. It will feel raw, and you will feel vulnerable. You may feel very wooden and not know how to be. Good. You don't want to be a drone anymore and it is worth this discomfort to find out who you could be. You will begin to find simple things much more enjoyable when you are worrying less about whether people like you and think you are acceptable. You won't be wasting your life force on pointless grovelling to people who probably aren't very interesting anyway.

However, whilst this all sounds straightforward, you will have to get past the jury in your mind to drop these people-pleasing ways. In *Being and Nothingness*, Sartre (1943) said that we can only become our true selves by decisively rejecting the identities imposed upon us by others. The people who have inadvertently contributed to your becoming a groveller live on in your mind, deciding when and to whom you must grovel. You can choose to dump them, but you will first have to admit they are there. If these relics live on in your mind, you will allow them to influence every interaction and experience you have.

The narcissists you have encountered (to whom we are now being extremely grateful) will each have a place on your jury. You have a new job, and whilst it is going well, your narcissistic ex-boss is in your mind and has decided you will be fired. You must try extra hard and so make endless cups of coffee and do everyone else's photocopying. You are going on a date, and your ex is in your mind telling you that you are a loser. You fawn and tell the date far too much about yourself, exchanging your life story for approval. You meet your friends for drinks, and the mean girl from school, who you haven't seen for 30 years, is telling you that you are ugly and your friends hate you. You believe it and buy more rounds of drinks than the others, hoping it will make them like you. Until you move these relics on, this will be your lot, experiencing everyone and everything through the filter of everyone who has hurt or shamed you in the past.

How do you begin to ditch or update the jury? If you've had therapy but were working with a counsellor who didn't explain forgiveness in a helpful way, you might think it's fine to hold on to the resentment. If you really want to, you can—but doing so will limit your life to the kind of trashy internal dialogues described in the previous paragraph. The narcissists are long gone and on to their next victim. You hold on to them because you don't see why they should get away with what they've done. But they are just a memory now, one that lives on in your mind.

You were bullied for ten years by your ex, and now you want to keep arguing with them in your head. You didn't get even with them in real life back then, and you certainly won't through imagined conversations now. Narcissists love arguing and don't fight fairly. They move the goalposts mid-discussion, twist the facts, and lie—so that a sensible resolution is rarely possible. Due to their lack of object constancy, they can't hold onto the idea that you mean anything to them during a disagreement. In that moment, you're either *all bad* or *all good*. When you are 'bad,' they feel entitled to say and do whatever they like to you. That is why arguing with a narcissist is pointless. Recognising this will benefit you immensely. You don't want to win a fight with someone who fights dirty. You're far better off acknowledging that this is *their* territory and walking away.

You may be able to let go of them one by one. You might picture yourself in a little boat on a river. You have multiple ropes, each attached to the boat of a past adversary. Pull one up into your mind and take a good look. See how small they are in your life now. Untie the rope and let their boat float on down the river and away from you into the night. Continue and pull the next one up into your mind. Untie the ropes one by one and feel the relief as you are now free from dragging them behind you. Know that it is over for you. They are people you experienced, and they do not define you. They have nothing to do with you now. You are floating into crystal-clear water, and the sun is shining. You have no one to argue with in your mind. Life is good.

If you feel the need to have other influences in your mind, pick some really good ones. If you have never had a healthy friendship of any sort, draw on someone who seems to be a good role model. When you are in a situation where you are about to grovel, and you feel tempted to consult the old relics, pull in the good influence instead. What do you think they might say in this situation? They certainly wouldn't recommend that you grovel. If you are considering dating again, read up on the warning signs of narcissism, and you could have the author on your jury. What would they think about what this date is saying? Are there red flags?

In this chapter, we have looked at why we should be grateful to all narcissists. They could be the only means by which people are waking up to the fact that they have been on wheels all their lives, pushed around by others. This is not something that a public service broadcast is going to cure because people don't seem to hear it when it is explained to them. I am speaking to you, the individual, to see if this resonates with you. I am asking that if you have experienced the wound of narcissistic abuse, you stay awake and act so that one more person begins to say no. Life is good when you are not a drone.

In the next chapters, we are going to look at ways in which you can build on this. If you are not being controlled or deferring to the other, how do you navigate the way forward?

Chapter 9

I Just Need to Love Myself. Right?

If you have at some point reached the stage of ditching the people-pleasing in order to become more self-led, you may have found it difficult to navigate the next steps. This might be because the general advice regarding how to move forward tends to be shaky. You will probably be told to love yourself and start looking into how you do that. However, this is difficult to get right. Unfortunately, many people, in the name of self-love, become as selfish as the narcissists they are trying to move on from. In this chapter, we will investigate why this might occur.

Of those who wake up to the fact they have been controlled all their lives, many will voice to others that things are going to change. They often say that previously they couldn't ask for what they wanted, but now they will. They will then proceed to expect the best bedroom on holiday, eat the last chocolate, talk over people and leave the dishes for someone else to do. They will proclaim that this is in the name of self-love and that they won't be trampled on any longer.

If this is you, it is important to consider the wider picture and not react as though you are finally going to take what you deserve. This is likely to be happening because you have not shifted the controllers from the jury in your mind. Consequently, when a situation arises that may have hitherto led you to make way for another, you now step forward and claim the prize. You are making it fair with the adversaries from your past who you are allowing to live on in your mind. They have nothing to do with the present, and you aren't getting even with them—they are long gone. What you are doing is irritating the current people in your life by punishing them for what has gone before.

When you were born, you had no doubt that you deserved to be or have your needs met. You were blissfully non-separate, part of the whole. This wonderful state was shattered with the realisation that your mother's milk did not just appear as soon as you wanted it.

Consequently, you developed a separate sense of self that needed to do something in order to get what it wanted. To survive, you developed an attachment style as you attuned to the behaviour of your primary caregiver. If she was secure within herself, you learned that your needs were usually met, even though you may have had to wait at times. However, if her attachment style was insecure, you would have needed to adjust your expectations and behaviours. If she was avoidant, you learned not to expect love or affection. If she was ambivalent, you learned to make noise to be heard. In the first year of your life, you will have learned to control or appease to get what you need or to do without.

Fast-forward to when you realise you have put yourself last all your life for no reason other than the computer being loaded with faulty software. Your conscious mind realises that you have been losing out. It hears from others that the antidote to this is self-love. The mind is a brilliant computer, but it can't love. What it does tell you to give yourself in the name of self-love will be based on ideas probably derived from movies, trashy novels or social media. Interestingly, this is the kind of love proffered by a narcissist during their love-bombing stage. This is why they use histrionic language and acts. They, too, have to make up what love might be with their minds as they don't have access to it either.

If you can't love yourself using your mind, where does love come from? Love is not a thing that you can magic up for anyone else or yourself. It is not an add-on. Psychiatrist and consciousness researcher David Hawkins (2012) described love as 'a way of being … the energy that radiates when the blocks to it have been surrendered'. There is no need to chase anything outside of yourself in order to get some love, and no need to love yourself. If love is a state that is naturally occurring within you, blocked only by your wrong thinking, then trying to love yourself is a bit nonsensical. That would be trying to add something when it is already occurring within you, like gold-plating a solid gold watch.

Every difficulty mentioned in this book so far is a block to accessing the energy that is love within you. In order for it to push up through, you will need to stop: trying to be liked; comparing yourself to others; being affronted by what others are saying;

ruminating on what you have said; hanging on to the hurts of the past; adding on new hurts and being resentful of self and others. As you relax and let go of all this garbage that is not you, so the pathway will be cleared for love to come through. It is unconditional and has nothing to do with falling in love. You will find yourself enraptured at the sight of wild geese flying over you or a fly walking across your windowsill. Your energy levels will soar as though you are powered by rocket fuel. It is as though you have finally taken your foot off the hosepipe.

Due to childhood conditioning, most people don't have access to this way of being and so understandably search for it in any way that they can. Indian guru Sadghuru (2020) explains that it is not love itself that is sought but the state of 'blissfulness' that love brings with it. Many will seek it in romantic relationships. The initial loved-up stage lasts six to 12 months, and people describe feeling as though they are walking on air. They are generally nicer to be around. They float above the hosepipe until the high wears off, and they begin to notice 'flaws' in their partner that the high had masked. For others, the feeling might be accessed via chemical means. Ecstasy users float above the hosepipe, loving everyone as the huge surge in serotonin elevates them above their usual inhibition, self-criticism and criticism of others. Alcohol lifts the drinker up off the hosepipe so that temporarily, self and others seem more fun and attractive. The dopamine hit derived from clicking 'buy now' on the internet gives shoppers a short but sweet lift.

Unfortunately, what goes up via external stimuli must come down. This will leave you feeling worse than before you got that hit. Then, the self-punishment begins so that the only way out is to get another dose of whatever gave you the brief interlude. If these methods haven't been working for you in the past, then how else can you begin to feel better?

Clients have been told by some counsellors to show themselves they are 'worth it' by buying themselves flowers or having a bubble bath. For someone who dislikes themselves, this is pointless. The self-loathing part will reject the gift because the meanness to self is its way of managing life, its distorted survival strategy. This part doesn't want gifts; it wants to feel hard done by.

Unless the client can forgive themselves, this part will prevent them from moving forward.

So, how do you start that process of forgiving yourself if everything you have experienced has led you to perceive yourself as a loser? I find it really helpful to tell clients what Indian guru, Sadghuru, teaches. He asks who you think you are to abuse the mind and body that you have been given to tend. I think that whatever your belief system, this is a pertinent question. You think that because they are yours, you can do what you like with them. It is, therefore, fine to continue the vile self-talk, be unhealthy, do a horrible and boring job and be in rubbish relationships. This poor mind and body are trapped with you running the show. They can't escape from you, so do you think you could be kinder to them? If you were treating anyone else like this, you would be arrested.

In *Psycho-Cybernetics*, one of the greatest self-help books of the 20th century, Maxwell Maltz (1960) reminds us that every species is engineered for success. Whilst humans aren't the only species able to imagine, they are the only ones able to utilise imagination to create new events and objects. Although this creative power is innate for all humans, negative early conditioning leads you to wrongly imagine that you are less than or a failure. If you can remember that all you have to do is return to the successful design that you really are, then the process now is just one of letting go of all the negative things you habitually tell yourself. You will need to be vigilant and not let yourself get away with the addictive negative self-talk. Back to the theme running through this book—only you are responsible for how you feel. Take responsibility and say, 'No more' to the nasty chatter.

Unfortunately, if you don't sort this out, your view of others will be just as negative. This is because every fault you find in yourself, you will be scanning for in others. However much you might protest it isn't true, you can only accept others to the extent that you accept yourself. Whatever criticisms, realistic or perceived, that you see in yourself will be reflected back at you in every interaction with every person. If you think you are stupid, your radar will be tracking for intelligence or stupidity in others. If you think you are too loud, you will home in on the volume of others' voices. Ram Dass (2014) described the process as 'polishing the mirror' so that one's growth involves increasingly seeing the wholeness in others reflected back in ourselves and, in turn, in others. There is no escape, and, like an algorithm on your social media, you will only perceive and receive what you are or think you are.

It is interesting that many people who consider themselves do-gooders quote the golden rule, 'Do unto others as you would have them do unto you'. This rule appears in some form in every religious text, so why does it not also apply to how one treats oneself? Perhaps because when these texts were written millennia ago, people hadn't been so conditioned to dislike themselves. Perhaps the golden rule needs updating for the self-loathing mind-set of the 21st century. It might read, 'Do *to **yourself and** others as you would have others do unto you'. This is really important because unless you get this, you will be a nuisance to yourself and all. If you are rushing to help and please others while secretly despising yourself, your view of them will be just as distorted as your view of yourself.

We have explored how the adaptation of people-pleasing coincides with losing touch with your own feelings and needs. Your crucial internal compass has been sidelined since childhood, and the task of deciding what you should do has long been outsourced to others. But the good news is that while the compass may have lain dormant, it has not been destroyed. As you stop berating yourself, self-acceptance begins to dissolve the need for external validation and the fawning can finally cease. When situations arise, you will begin to resist the drug of pleasing others and realise that you can say no. From out of the ashes, your self-worth begins to re-emerge.

You had shoved your own feelings and needs under a trapdoor, focusing instead on what you thought others needed, often to your own detriment. Now, you have the choice to open that door and allow those long-buried feelings to rise. All the narcissists who hurt you remain stuck in the same place they were when you entered their lives. Their ability to learn from experience is blocked, because their sense of self is too fragile for them to dare open their own trapdoor. You are fortunate to be willing and able to face what has been buried. This is what allows real self-worth to develop: a self-worth that isn't dependent on the approval of others.

If you feel envious of a narcissistic ex who seems to have moved on quickly with a new partner, take that as a signal that there is still healing work for you to do. It's not enviable that they appear to move on so easily—it's a tragedy. The real affliction is that their trapdoor has been snapped shut and sealed with cement. While this may shield them from feelings of emptiness and despair, it also prevents them from ever accessing true self-esteem or love. Their next relationship will be just another miserable repeat of the one they had with you.

So, let's say you are willing to open your trapdoor. This means you are willing to accept that the past needn't define you. It means that you are willing to feel what comes up, good or bad. Ideally, if you are having therapy, the therapist will help you to experience the feelings and move forward. However, many therapists and people in the helping professions describe themselves with pride as 'wounded-healers'. This is problematic as, firstly, a therapist is not a healer. Secondly, in advertising the wound, there is pride in the trauma.

Whilst we are closely studying in this book how trauma can be transformative, we have also looked at how important it is for the therapist to see beyond it. If the therapist's own self-concept is that of a wounded healer, how will they ever see you going beyond your wounds? How many years of work on themselves has this wounded healer done in order to still refer to themselves as wounded? Would you book in with someone who advertised themselves as the 'injured chiropractor' or 'bankrupt accountant'?

If you are still with me in this book, I hope that you already have an understanding that crystallising your identity around the worst of your past is limiting. Whilst social media is helpful for increasing people's understanding of their mental health, it also encourages people to become well-known for their mental health difficulties and negative life experiences. You are not your trauma; you are not your experiences. If you think you are, then you will continue to see yourself as defined by them. What were you before the trauma? Nothing?

I explain it to clients using the plant in the counselling room. The plant is expanding into the world being a plant. It does not use its precious energy arguing with itself about how awful the shop was that it started out in, how much better the other plants were or how rotten I am compared to other plant owners. Humans, on the other hand, use most of their energy arguing internally about everything and everyone that has displeased or upset them. All of the plant's life force is emanating up through it as it unfolds as a plant into the world in all its magnificence. Unfortunately, your life force has been splintering off around pockets of old hurts since you were a child. Each time an event or person has disappointed you in some way over your lifespan so far, more energy has been syphoned off to keep these hurts suppressed. It is only when you are willing to feel them and let them pass through you that they will dissolve and your energy will be restored to its rightful usage.

In order to begin to discover what you could be, it is essential to let go of all the stories you tell yourself about who you are. These stories are addictive and hard to give up because you think they define you. These stories are what give you permission to grip on to all of the old hurts you have suppressed. They are what allow your energy to be misdirected towards each and every one of these fossils. You will need to be strict with yourself and know that you are the one now harming yourself. You are in charge. You are the boss. It is time to use your awareness to watch what you are up to.

Like an investigator, you are going to start watching the workings of your mind, looking for patterns. Initially, it is enough to be a spy. However, as you begin to recognise that internally, you are like a scratched record, repeating the same old stuff, it becomes harder to let yourself get away with it. It becomes tedious when you are on to it. Just why are you telling yourself such repetitive and boring stories about yourself?

If your mind is repeating the old stuff and getting in your way, take charge and remove your awareness to another place. Louise Hay's 'All is well in my world' (Hay, 2024) is a really simple statement to use when you are feeling yourself go into panic or a low. You are not denying there is panic, but you are focusing on something else while it passes, because it will pass. Parent yourself like you would soothe a child if they were panicking about school or friends. Tell yourself all is well. Be firm and keep repeating it in a calm and soothing tone. Know that you are in charge of your internal world, and if you make that more joyful, you will be joyful.

You may be able to further help yourself using humour as you become more familiar with the parts of you that you have been pushing down. If you have been grovelling to someone and become aware of it, picture yourself bowing down, saying, 'Yes, master; anything you say, master'. If someone shook their fist at you when driving, say, 'Thank you so much', and laugh it off. Don't let any more of this garbage be locked into your storehouse, ready to come up and haunt you in the future. The more positive your reaction to it in the present, the less likely it will be to revisit it in the future. Bat it away with joy.

We have looked at how you might navigate the early stages once you have realised that you don't want to be controlled anymore. We have looked at how it is possible to start to feel good from within as the blockages to the natural energy that is within you are removed. When you were born, you had full access to that energy. It wasn't until the conditioning by misinformed others began that you lost touch with it. You got the wrong impression and began to believe that love is something that needs a particular person or condition to be felt. You also wrongly believed that you are limited to be that which both prior experience had suggested and others had assumed you to be.

So, if you are not limited in the way that you had previously assumed yourself to be, how do you try out new ways of being? What could your life look like, and how might you get on the path to that way of living? In the closing chapters, we are going to investigate whether it is possible to create the kind of life you would like to live. We are going to start by looking at the fact that you are already creating your reality, whether you like it or not!

Chapter 10
Manifest. Can I Have It All?

I didn't really want to include this word in this book, but there isn't a more accurate word to use in its place, so I will be using it. I was loath to use it because there are so many people offering expensive courses online, making outlandish promises regarding manifesting. Anyone offering one particular method and saying it will deliver results either doesn't understand what they are talking about or is being economical with the truth. In tandem with this, the majority of people who try out any of the techniques only dabble in them and then say they don't work. This combination of shoddy teaching and half-hearted learning has resulted in the negative view held by many of this naturally occurring mechanism.

If we return to the theme of wanting something for nothing that we looked at in earlier chapters, unfortunately, the law of attraction predominantly attracts people with this kind of unrealistic thinking. We looked at how narcissists and the people-pleasers they are drawn to are searching for someone to magic away their self-loathing. It doesn't work and isn't sustainable. Similarly, many of the people hanging around in the law of attraction community are looking for a quick fix with little input. Say a few affirmations, and you will be rich; imagine you are an artist, and it will happen. It is obvious that this is unrealistic.

The law of attraction is simple, but it is difficult to action successfully. You will get what you are or what you believe yourself to be. End of. This is demonstrated most clearly in the relationships of a narcissist. They create a false persona in order to attract the kind of partner they think they want. Once they have found a suitable target, they action their plan with love-bombing. The partner they attract has low self-esteem and feels very fortunate indeed to be so attractive to this charming person. They are a perfect match in their self-loathing and the belief that someone else can fix it. The narcissist uses smoke and mirrors to keep the partner trapped until they can bear no more, and the relationship implodes. They withdraw to regroup, both parties saying how rotten the other was and how they lied about who they were. It is only if either side is able to see that they are attracting what they believe about themselves that they will be able to climb off the circular train track.

This book is about how to manage your mind so that you feel good and your life improves. This is why I am including manifesting. You don't actually have to do anything to manifest—you are already doing it, as seen in the previous paragraph. You will get in life what you believe you are. Unfortunately, due to childhood conditioning and not having known that it is possible to manage the mind, you will have limiting beliefs about yourself. These beliefs form your identity; who you think you are. If you believe you are someone who people don't like much, you will form habits that relate to that belief. You might, for instance, avoid socialising and this habit will lead to you not meeting people. This will confirm to you that you are not popular and that people dislike you.

If you are someone with anxiety and, in particular, if you also have ADHD, you will probably start a new job convinced that it will go wrong. Whatever you believe about yourself will echo off the walls of the office to be absorbed back into you, confirming what you believe to be true. With ADHD, imposter syndrome leads to the belief that people will find out that you don't know what you are doing.

You start the job. The boss comes in on day two and doesn't give you such a big smile as yesterday. Oh no, she is already beginning to realise you aren't equipped for the role. You try harder but feel resentful and stressed because everyone else seems so relaxed. However, they don't talk to you in the same way they do to each other. They obviously don't like you. You start doing more for them than they do for you and the resentment builds. You begin stomping around the office and giving monosyllabic answers. You are called in for a chat with the boss because they aren't sure you are right for the role. This was manifesting at its most effective. However, you manifested what you didn't want using your imagination.

So, if it is this easy for you to manifest what you don't want, could it be this easy to manifest what you do want? The short answer is yes, but the reality is that it takes a huge commitment to change who you think you are and therefore what you attract. It requires stopping the denial. It requires being vigilant regarding your thinking every moment of every day. No slacking, no quick fixes and definitely not something for nothing. It requires not telling yourself stories about yourself and others. It requires dropping your past. If you believe that you are your experiences and identify with them, that is what you will be attracting more of. End of.

If you had thought that the law of attraction was mystical and for new-age hippies, you might rethink seeing it from this perspective. You're doing it anyway, but if you hadn't realised this, you'd have been attracting all manner of unwanted consequences. In each of the chapters of this book so far, the methods regarding tidying up the mind are applicable to helping attract what you would like in your life. If you can: address your anxiety; manage what you download to your subconscious; stop being ruled by your feelings; stop wanting something for nothing; parent yourself so that you don't look for others to do it; stop the people-pleasing; stop controlling or being controlled—then you are well on your way to being able to manifest what you would like in your life. Not mystical, but no mean feat.

The law of attraction was popularised in the mid-19th century by movements such as those of American New Thought in the US and by the Theosophical Society in the UK. The ideas were a revival of those found in ancient scriptures of all denominations. New Thought preachers reintroduced the idea that thoughts and beliefs not only affect the person internally but will play out to become the person's reality. These movements encouraged people to begin to challenge the way that they used their minds, warning of the perils of negative thinking. A number of methods were taught to help people heal themselves or change their lives for the better.

If you don't like the fact that the aforementioned influences are all based on ancient religious texts, don't switch off yet. Using these methods within a purely psychological framework is also effective. At the same time as New Thought was emerging in the US, hypnosis was also a developing science. The French psychologist and hypnotist Émile Coué developed his form of 'self-healing' in the early 20th century. The basis of his work was the understanding that any healing that has ever taken place has only been able to do so because of the power of autosuggestion. The person being healed has complete faith in the ability to be healed and is, therefore healed. Hence why the placebo effect is so common. Coué taught his patients to be able to use autosuggestion and heal themselves.

Coué said, 'Whenever imagination and will come into conflict, it is always imagination that triumphs' (cited in Grimes, 2017, p. 42). Someone will say every day that they are determined to give up smoking, but if they believe that they can't quit, they will continue to smoke. It is not effort that makes them give up but the belief that it can be done. This is really important and ties in with all of the previous chapters concerning our thoughts. Whilst we don't choose our thoughts, what we believe about ourselves will set the frequency for the kind that we attract. If you are allowing your conscious mind to run with thoughts about how useless you are all day, then the subconscious will believe it and act accordingly. It is a faithful, unquestioning servant. It will do whatever you keep running by it, so you had better check what you are telling it!

Coué said, 'Whatever we think comes true for us. We, therefore, must not think anything detrimental to ourselves' (cited in Grimes, 2017, p.122). Whilst you may not want to believe this, it is this belief that underpinned his extremely successful work. Coué helped thousands of people cure themselves from physical and mental illnesses such as asthma, insomnia, tuberculosis, cancer and many more.

If you want to succeed in life and feel good, it is essential that your conscious mind gives the message to your subconscious that you are able to achieve and you can succeed in your life. There is no point in daydreaming about a great job if you think you are useless. It is pointless searching for a partner if you believe you aren't worth dating. Hoping you will be rich one day is a waste of time if you believe money will always be an issue for you. Your conscious mind is the gatekeeper to the subconscious and it is time to take responsibility for what you are allowing to be impressed upon the subconscious. What seeds are you sowing in yours?

Coué's simple method is described brilliantly in two concise books: *Self-Mastery Through Conscious Autosuggestion* (Coué, 1922/2006) and *Simple Self-Healing* (Grimes, 2017). The editor of the latter text, Tim Grimes, is an expert on Coué and discusses how to use Coué's method, as well as other methods, in his podcast 'The Law of Attraction Explored' on Spotify and on his YouTube channel. The method is based on the Law of Reverse Effort. We very easily program our subconscious for failure by the constant drip-feed of interminable worry. It is effortless. Flip this effortless negativity on its head and instead drip-feed positive thoughts into the subconscious. It is so simple it is laughable.

So, you can see that the law of attraction is really only the managing of the subconscious mind through the use of the conscious mind. As New Thought preacher Joseph Murphy (1963) describes beautifully in *The Power of the Subconscious Mind*, 'Your subconscious mind is always expressing, reproducing, and manifesting according to your habitual thinking'. Your habitual thinking is compulsive. Feeling sorry for yourself is addictive. Many of the people who try out the law of attraction will spend time on the affirmations or visualisations but struggle to manage the mind throughout the day. Many meditate endlessly but cannot manage the most basic challenges arising in front of them. The great spiritual teacher J Krishnamurti said meditation 'relates to our everyday activities' (https://kfoundation.org/meditation). Sitting cross-legged in a corner for hours is secondary to being able to navigate the events of the day without reacting according to your old stuff.

If you are a messy person and are affirming that you are a tidy person, it is no good carrying on as you always have done. If you really would like to be a tidy person, then, to start with, you might pick just one aspect of tidiness to work on. Change the habit, and you will change your identity. Your identity is only what you think you are according to what kind of things you do. So, why not pick up your dirty laundry from the floor each day and put it in the laundry basket?

You can then say to yourself that you are the kind of person who does pick up their laundry. Keep affirming and you will find that you eventually add in another relevant habit, such as washing your dishes. Live as if you are a tidy person and bit by bit, it will materialise.

Many people give up affirmations, whether written or spoken, saying that they haven't worked or that things got worse. In my own experience and from reading the experiences of well-known New Thought preachers, you can expect anything to happen. This is because in order for something to shift, other factors around it need to be reordered.

An example might be that you are affirming that you have good relationships with all your colleagues. You are probably affirming this because you struggle with workplace relationships and want an improvement. You may find, for example, that you lose your job quite quickly and then stop affirming because this isn't what you ordered. However, if you ride it out, you will find that it took this loss in order for you to find a job with nicer colleagues. In addition, the loss of the job will make you more grateful for the next job so that you might address the difficulties *you* were bringing to your workplace relationships.

Back to one of the recurring themes in this book: if you expect something for nothing from affirming you could end up in a worse place than before. As seen in the last paragraph, if you resent the bumps and crunches needed to happen to give you what you want, you will fall at the first post. Instead, remind yourself that the more you can accept what is unfolding in front of you with gratitude, the greater your ability to ride the wave.

Take responsibility for everything you face whilst keeping up the affirmations. Know that you are headed in the right direction and are accepting of the bumps in the path. Remember that for the law of attraction to work in your favour, you have to be the kind of person who could have this new aspect in their life. Events will occur that give you the opportunity to become that person if you don't resist them, but instead learn from them.

In this chapter, we have looked at what manifesting is, and how, if you address the issues talked about in the preceding chapters, it will become easier for you to lead the kind of life you would like to live. We have looked at how manifesting is more straightforward as a concept than many people realise. You are doing it whether you like it or not, so you may as well do it so that you are attracting good into your life rather than more turmoil. In the next chapter, we will look at a really important question regarding the use of these techniques: How do you know what you want?

Chapter 11

How Do I Know What I Want?

If you ask someone what they want, they will want to avoid what they don't like and have more of what they do like. However, these likes and dislikes are derived from prior experience. Humans will look for experiences that make them feel safe and secure based on that which has occurred before. You may wonder what is wrong with that, but if the mind can only choose from prior experience, isn't that a bit limiting?

If you have been bullied at school, you might say you want a house away from schools so that you aren't reminded of your past. If you have grown up without money and feel ashamed of this, you may want to be rich. Perhaps you have always felt unattractive and so long for a partner who will find you attractive. You may feel that no one is interested in what you say and feel desperate to be listened to. All of these wants are based on unresolved childhood issues. You feel that if only these were fixed, life would be really good for you.

However, let's say that you get any of these wishes fulfilled. On their own, what good are they? You have a house away from schools, but the bullying still lives on unresolved in your mind. Your world has become smaller, but the problem remains. You might attract money but don't feel comfortable in luxurious locations because you don't feel you fit in. You find a partner who says you are attractive to them, but you don't believe them because you still despise how you look. You get bookings to speak at conferences but are waiting to be found out for the fool that you are.

Your conscious mind has got you into this mess by wrong thinking. You have believed that you are your experiences and are now trying to visualise and affirm a fix for this wrong thinking. Therefore, you are trying to get out of the mess that your conscious mind has created using the limited conscious mind that has created the mess. However, you will be very pleased to know that all of the preceding chapters of this book point to ways out of this quagmire. Your way out is by letting go of all of the old hurts, resentments, and comparisons to others. You don't want to have money so that you can stop feeling inferior. Wouldn't you like to have money so that you lead a good life? You don't want to speak at conferences to not seem like a fool. Wouldn't you like to have something so important to say that you can't wait to say it, whatever the reception? You don't want to hide from schools. Wouldn't you like to be choosing a house because you love both it and its location?

However, let's say you do come up with some ideas that aren't based on old hurts. Perhaps you do recognise that you would like a good life and feel that money will help you in its pursuit. Are you the kind of person who would be able to live a good life with money? Is your identity constructed from habits that will benefit from a surge in wealth? If you have a tendency to shop excessively, you will find yourself wasting more money; if you have a taste for alcohol, you might work less and frequent bars more; if you overeat, you will get more takeouts. If you haven't sorted out your compulsions, an increase in wealth will expand the glitches.

We looked at the work of Émile Coué in the last chapter. He recognised that because the subconscious mind oversees our mental and physical functions, it is better qualified than the conscious mind to recognise what would be beneficial for us (cited in Grimes, 2017, p.110). This was his reason for devising a one-size-fits-all autosuggestion: 'Every day, in every way, I'm getting better and better'. This leads to growth that is balanced and befitting the design of the individual in all their uniqueness. In contrast, the conscious mind is more likely to create a 'Frankenstein' type of growth as it compares itself to others and attempts to match up to or outdo them.

For instance, Frederick Dodson (2014), who teaches the Reality Creation Technique, describes having in his younger years successfully manifested being irresistible to women *with horrendous results.* He was continually pestered by women he wasn't interested in, who said they were in love with him. He hadn't understood that the emotion behind this goal was that of feeling insecure around women. Realising this enabled him to modify the intention to that of feeling confident in the presence of women.

For this reason, if you think you desire something, it is always important to ask yourself why you want it. A safer way to start is to work on the improvement of your relationship with both yourself and others. If you are able to forgive yourself and those you have held on to resentment toward, you will notice benefits in all areas of your life. If you haven't done this, your manifesting will relate to showing others that you are worth something or proving that you are successful. This will lead you to pursue goals that may not suit you at all and make your growth lopsided.

If you have an ongoing issue with a family member, for instance, you might use a technique based on that described by Neville Goddard (1956/2023, p.593). You might imagine the relation writing you a letter saying that the issue is resolved. It helps to actually picture the person writing and the words forming on the page. Imagine that it is a kind and loving letter, and feel the joy you would feel should you receive it. Neville recommended doing this whilst falling asleep, but it also works in your waking hours. What is essential is that you feel as good as you would feel should the situation be sorted. It is helpful to repeat this process for a number of days.

You might still be thinking this is unrealistic, but it tallies with findings in neuroscience. In the mid-20th century, Donald Hebb (1949, cited in Science Direct, 2020) discovered that 'neurons that fire together wire together'. With the example in the previous paragraph, when you had previously thought of this person, you pictured them as being difficult. Your whole body would have tensed at the thought of this, and you would have felt anxious, angry or both. The longer the situation continued, the deeper the neural pathway would have been trodden. However, as you picture the person in a positive light and the situation as being sorted, a new neural pathway is being laid down. If you continue to practise this method, the way in which you view this person will change, and if you come into contact with them, you will be more relaxed. A positive outcome is much more likely with you acting calm and friendly.

Another way in which you might practise positively manifesting change in your life is to tackle something that you find difficult. If you are a nervous driver, you will tense up each time you think about driving. You might devise a suitable affirmation, such as 'I drive competently and joyfully'. You might also use another Neville Goddard visualisation technique (therealityrevolution.com, 2019) whereby you imagine yourself in the future, telling someone about how you used to be afraid of driving. It needs to be realistic and use as many of your senses as possible. For instance, it could be in your sitting room, talking to your friend whilst you drink coffee together. Say to your friend that you remember when you were scared of driving. You might be smiling and laughing together. They might be saying that you always were a good driver but you just hadn't realised it. You will be imagining yourself driving really well now and finding it so easy.

This process is the same backwards process as we looked at in Chapter 9 when looking into the origins of love. I discussed how love isn't something to be added on from external stimuli but rather a state to be returned to as you discard that which you are not. Similarly, by this process, you are letting go of resentment and fear so that your natural state of 'I am' and 'I can' are able to come through. I am not the person who falls out with others, and I am not the person who is scared of driving. I am something that is aware of those ways that I can be if I believe my stories about my past. The more I can return to that something the better my life will become. It is not the case that this process will be difficulty-free. As we previously looked at, any change in how you would like to be will necessitate the repositioning of events and others around you.

Can you not, then, ask for what you would like to add to your life in the same way? You can, but it is not your conscious mind that is going to know what is best suited to your design or how far you could go. In *The Power of Your Subconscious Mind*, Joseph Murphy (1963) described how the conscious, objective mind deals with objects in the world, perceived via the five senses. This view is limited to that which you have already experienced. In contrast, the subconscious, subjective mind houses memory and emotion and perceives via intuition or the sixth sense. Murphy describes how many geniuses—physicists, actors, artists, and composers—have said they didn't consciously think up their best work. Inste[ad, after] years of imagining and searching for truth, the concepts see[m to] arrive fully formed.

This highlights an additional vital aspect regarding t[he] relationship between the conscious and subconscious mind. It is true that what you believe with your conscious mind will be impressed onto the subconscious and materialise in your life. However, once you are able to understand yourself more and tidy up your beliefs, your conscious mind will become quieter. There will be less noise from the constant chattering of anxiety and the low drone of depression. You will not be directing the ship towards expected doom with continual negative thinking, but will have a mind that is more open to the possibility of new frontiers and good outcomes.

This is crucial. Up until this point, with your conscious mind, you have been in conversation with parts of yourself you believed to be telling the truth. Anxiety masquerades as intuition, and you were believing everything it drip-fed you. You have a flight booked in and get a feeling you shouldn't get on the plane—is it anxiety or intuition? You have a feeling about your new neighbour and want to avoid them. Anxiety or intuition? You have applied for that job but have a feeling that it won't work out. Anxiety or intuition?

Sort out your anxiety, and all of this fake intuition will be dead in the water. From deep within the silence, you will begin to hear the whisperings of true intuition. You will begin to experience the beauty of the interdependent relationship of the heart and mind. The subconscious is often referred to as the heart, and the conscious as the mind. Hitherto, your mind (conscious) was listening to your anxiety and couldn't hear what your heart (subconscious) was trying to say. From your early childhood conditioning, you turned away from the heart and blocked out its voice. You were trained to listen to others' opinions regarding what was best for you.

Your heart knows it has a finite amount of time to communicate its wishes to you before you die. It is crying out for you to hear what it would like to do. As your conscious mind stills and you begin to listen, your heart will begin to sing with joy. The rewards kpot hits the jackpot. Eureka! This is when you live a joyful and meaningful life, whatever

ability to relax the greater will be your ability with your subconscious. Most people believe that . means watching television, reading newspapers or ..aying computer games. True relaxation involves dropping any resistance to life and letting go of all that could possibly concern you. If you have ever been hypnotised, this is the state you are looking for. If you would like a recorded meditation, Frederick Dodson's (2019) 'Deep relaxation in 10 minutes' is one of the best I have found for finding that state quickly. You may also find the meditations in the book *Psycho-Cybernetics* by Maxwell Maltz (1960) helpful. They are easy ways to fall into a very deep level of relaxation. There are many other ways of doing this, such as my affirmation video, which, through exercise and repetition, leads to a relaxed good feeling. The more that you practise, the more instantaneous the benefits become. Decision-making is improved, and anxiety reduced.

This is why the answers to seemingly insoluble problems often appear on waking after sleep. The conscious mind has been off-duty, but the subconscious never sleeps and without the limitations of the conscious mind, the answer has been able to arise from this infinite vault. It is a useful practice to ask your subconscious to send you an answer to a problem before you go to sleep. Many inventors, business leaders and creatives say that they rest during the day to find the answers to problems. If you are able to do this during a busy day, it will be a gold mine for you.

As you become a more relaxed person, your ability to focus and produce excellent work will increase. Your attention won't be wasted on nonsensical and repetitive thinking. You will begin to be nudged towards new skills and ventures by your heart. You might suddenly decide to learn a language or start dancing classes. You might hear someone talking about their job and think that you want to do something like that. You might start a new business.

Just go with it and see what happens. If it is a nudge from within, you won't be doing it to become famous or to become the best and beat the rest. You will be doing it for the doing of it and it will feel good. You won't care how others are doing it or compare yourself to them because you will be doing it according to your design. This is because it has naturally pushed out into the world from within you. You will not need to be encouraged to do these things. Your very life force will be driving them and you will be learning with the excitement and energy of a child. This is when you will be able to truly reparent yourself. You will take yourself by the hand and say, 'Yes, you can do this and I will help you to put the effort in and to keep practising until you get the hang of it'.

It is at this point, if you want to add the superpower of manifesting techniques, that you might add them into the mix. You are reparenting yourself, helping yourself to be patient and put in the hard work. Simultaneously, you will use your imagination to visualise yourself succeeding in whatever it is that you have chosen. You might say to yourself, 'Every day, in every way, I am improving at this'.

You make sure that you aren't going for a big prize or the outcome; you are in it for the journey and will be delighted wherever it goes. This is because you are expanding outwards into the world exactly as you should be, and everything is occurring around you exactly as it should be. No resistance, no complaining. You are getting on with it and are so grateful to be a guest on this planet.

Remember that if you want to become a particular way of being and begin to affirm or visualise that, you must be ready to become it immediately. You are throwing the ball in a particular direction and you are going to have to run to be able to catch it when it falls. You may find that where you are able to run falls far short of the ball's landing position. You may feel that you didn't ask to arrive at this point. Trust in the process and keep going. These obstacles appear as an opportunity for you to learn and change. It will take as long as it takes for you to become the person you want to be. You can only attract what you are, and so until you are ready to be it, you won't be.

As quoted by the Buddha, *"Events happen, deeds are done, there is no individual doer thereof."* Remember this, and you can't go far wrong. Yes, it is important to get yourself tidy on the inside—and that is the only thing you truly *can* change. But at the same time, you are a tiny speck in the vast mechanism of the whole. This perspective can be helpful when you're tempted to feel anxious or moody. After all, what difference does your tensing up really make to the unfolding of this incredible creation?

Chapter 12
BONUS CHAPTER
Reprogram Your Mind

If you would like to kick-start the process of letting go of some of the old rubbish that is preventing you from feeling good, then this is the chapter for you. I am giving you a tool that will blast away the gnarly crust of old miseries and allow you to access the energy that you have been blocking.

In each of the chapters so far, we have looked at how our minds become conditioned to negative thinking. This isn't an exercise in positive thinking—it is a reset to your natural state of feeling good. The affirmations are to remind you that: you are programmed for success; you can drop resentment towards self and others; and that the universe is one of abundance, not lack. Gratitude is mentioned throughout the routine and is an essential component of any affirmations.

This method has so many benefits that if you try it, you will begin to look forward to your appointment with yourself each day:

- The combination of exercising and affirming is very powerful. The subconscious is at its most receptive when you are relaxed, and exercise is one of the most effective ways to induce a relaxed state.

- It will set your mood to a good one every morning. Your mood is like a transistor radio setting and will attract positive or negative thoughts according to the frequency. This practice will improve your frequency substantially.

- It will generate new brain cells because you will be jumping up and down.

- It will create new neural pathways because you are repeating messages regarding forgiveness, success, and abundance to yourself over and over again, overwriting the old negative beliefs.

- You will be doing arm movements that go with the affirmations, giving them even more meaning. This will further increase your belief that they are true.

- The arm movements will tone up your arms in a remarkable way.

- You will be saying the affirmations, hearing the affirmations, and seeing your lips move while they are said to you by you. This combination is very effective for downloading the affirmations to your subconscious mind.

- You will be talking while running and jumping, which will improve your fitness.

- You will have fun every morning.

- This is a full 30 minutes of reprogramming your subconscious mind, carried out before you even begin your day.

If you'd like to follow the routine I do each morning, you can find the video on YouTube: https://youtu.be/HE_rjrzr54Y

I have listed below the affirmations that I currently do each morning and explained each one and its source, if not made up by me:

1. Good morning (insert your name) I love you.

You may find this first affirmation the most difficult to say. When Louise Hay (2016) worked with clients, she would ask them to look in the mirror and say to themselves, 'I love you'. Many would need to start with a modified version, such as 'I am learning to like you' because for the majority, self-disdain is the norm. Although the exercise might seem simplistic, it is powerful and cuts like a knife. All the aspects of ourselves that we use as excuses not to move forward are flushed out. People will say, for example, that they are too stupid; ugly; old; boring; overweight etc to be able to love themselves. Whatever comes up for you, just acknowledge it and be aware of self-love as a concept that is achievable. Forgive yourself for whatever faults you think you have and forgive yourself for having punished yourself for these perceived faults. If you are punishing yourself while doing this affirmation, forgive yourself for that too.

2. Health, Success, Wealth, Success.

Joseph Murphy explains that when beginning to affirm, saying 'I am wealthy' can cause the conscious mind to argue with the affirmation. He suggests that dropping the 'I' pronoun allows the conscious mind to accept this new information.

3. Today is better than yesterday. Tomorrow will be better than today.

This has been attributed to a number of sources. It is a useful affirmation to say throughout the day.

4. Everything is unfolding exactly as it should.

From spiritual teacher Robert Adams (*Silence of the Heart*, 2006). As events unfold throughout the day, whatever they are, this helps with acceptance and the ability to respond with agility.

5. I am born to win, I am born to succeed. Thank you, thank you, thank you.

This is a Joseph Murphy affirmation.

6. I've banished the doubt. I've flushed it out.

Many New Thought teachers talk about banishing doubt. Know that self-doubt is the basis of all procrastination. Drop it and act now.

7. The following meditation will bring many wonderful things into your life. Listen to it and say: These truths are sinking into my subconscious mind. I picture them going from my conscious to my subconscious like seeds deposited in the soil. I know I create my own destiny. My faith is in the infinite being which created all things and my faith in God is my

fortune. This means an abiding faith in all things good. I live in the joyous expectancy of the best and only the best comes to me. I know the harvest I will reap in the future because all my thoughts are God's thoughts and the power of God is with my thoughts of good. My thoughts are the seeds of goodness, truth, beauty and abundance. I now place my thoughts of love, peace, joy, success, abundance, security, goodwill in the garden of my mind. This is God's garden. The glory and beauty of God will be expressed in my life and I know my garden will yield an abundant harvest. From this moment forward, I express life, love, truth. I am radiantly happy and prosperous in all my ways and God multiplies my good exceedingly.

From: How to Manifest Your Best Life, Dr Joseph Murphy (Timeless Knowledge, 2022). As you are saying this, imagine your mind as a beautiful garden in which you are planting these seeds for an abundant and successful life.

8. I have a happy, safe, healthy, wealthy, harmonious, joyful, successful family. Thank you.

I picture my two daughters and myself and us all looking really happy.

9. I own a lovely home, in a beautiful village, in a wonderful world in an abundant universe. Thank you.

It doesn't matter if you don't own your home—if you would like to, then affirm it. If you would rather live in a city or by the sea, then adjust the affirmation accordingly.

10. You love, you are love, you are loved. I love, I am love, I am loved. We love, we are love, we are loved.

I am affirming, both for myself and the other.

11. I forgive, I am forgiven. You forgive, you are forgiven.

Forgiveness of self and others is an essential basis for feeling good. Whilst affirming this you can think of anyone you might be resenting and forgive them.

12. I've let all the pain and anger wash away. It's not me, it's not mine, it's not you, it's not yours.

We are not our trauma or experiences, good or bad. Let it all wash off you and others you might think of.

13. Guilt and resentment are a thing of the past. Forgive myself and others and it makes me grow fast.

Growth will be lopsided if you are holding on to resentment towards self or others. Choose to let go and let yourself grow.

14. I only expect the best in life and the best is what I get. Health, wealth, joy, abundance, freedom. Thank you, God. It's raining money and prosperity on me. I'm so grateful, I'm so free.

This will help switch your mindset from one of lack to one of abundance.

15. I am a magnet for money, prosperity of every kind is drawn to me. I am a magnet for money. The river of abundance is flowing through me. I am a magnet for money. Prosperity of every kind is drawn to me. I am a magnet for money. I'm so grateful, I'm so free.

As you are affirming this, imagine the river of abundance flowing through you.

16. My income increases every year. Of course it does.

Before getting into any of this, I found that I was having to pay more tax at the end of each year because my earnings had increased more than expected. I often said, 'My income increases every year, so I must be prepared this year and save more for tax'. It is a good example of the subconscious accepting what the conscious says to it. Interestingly, I was saying it in a grumbling way due to tax. Now, I say it and celebrate the increase in tax every year.

17. I have a lavish, steady, dependable income, consistent with integrity and mutual benefit.

This is the American physicist Robert Millikan's affirmation, which I came across in Neville Goddard's (1949/2023 p. 351) teachings.

18. Every day in every way, I'm growing wealthier and wealthier.

Based on Émile Coué's work and bringing in the necessity of being kind to self when difficulty arises.

19. Every day I soar higher and higher. Every day I soar higher and higher. If I take a hit, I love myself more and soar higher than ever before.

Based on Émile Coué's work.

20. Invisible supply, present within and through me in each and every moment. All my needs are taken care of. I know exactly what to do.

This has come together from a number of truths.

21. All my needs are taken care of.

Joseph Murphy, Louise Hay.

22. There is only love or fear. I choose love, love. There is only expand or contract. I expand, expand. Every time I get knocked back, I get myself back on track, with love, love. I've thrown away the stick I used to beat myself with. I get myself back on track with love, love.

This is based on the book *The Lazy Man's Guide to Enlightenment* by Thaddeus Golas (1972). In it he says that if you make mistakes, be kind to yourself. This is good advice. Children don't learn from punitive criticism, and neither do adults. It is kindness and encouragement that promote growth.

23. I love this skin I think I'm in. I love this mind I think is mine. I tend this seed built to succeed. To myself I'm kind and then I find that I feel good, of course I would. Hooray!

I mentioned earlier in the book that Sadghuru asks people who they think they are to abuse their minds and bodies. This is from the understanding that it is only you who can take care of yourself, as you are living with yourself. It is a great responsibility to take care of this being.

24. As I let go and surrender, free-fall, back into the life force from whence I came, all my problems are dissolved, all my pathways paved with gold. Thank you for your grace.

This is based on David Hawkins' (2012) *Letting Go*—in order to feel better, we need to face our emotions rather than avoid them. By doing so, we can let go, and as we repeat this process, we become freer. The second part is derived from Richard Dotts' (2016) *Dissolve the Problem*. The phrase 'All my pathways are paved with gold' is inspired by the work of motivational author and speaker Anthony Norvell.

25. I feel good, so life is good. The better I feel, the better life gets.

All law of attraction thinking points to this. If you wait until life gets better to feel better, you will be waiting a long time and be a victim of circumstance. Feeling good requires tidying up your mind first; then, your life will begin to change around that.

26. Today I dance on the grave of who I think I am. I'm free, I'm free, I'm free from being me.

If we get stuck in an identity, we become defensive of that person we believe ourselves to be and sensitive to criticism. The more you are able to let go of who you think you are, the better your life will become.

It is important to warm up before the routine and cool down after. The best pre and post run videos I have found are by yoga teacher, Joelle. They are really enjoyable stretches:

Warm-up: Joelle's 5-Min Yoga for Runners [https://www.youtube.com/watch?v=vU7cmYI8AFE]

Cool-down: Joelle's Post-Run Sequence [https://www.youtube.com/watch?v=z9FEh5o36NM]

The exercise doesn't have to be running. You could walk on the spot, row, use an exercise bike, trampoline or any form of exercise you would like. What matters most is that you are looking in the mirror as you do the affirmations.

You may think this sounds boring, but if you are serious about cleaning up your mind, I am afraid that process does require work. Your mind has been running itself badly for years and it will take some effort to get it back in shape.

Once you know the affirmations, your mind may wander. The next challenge is to keep your attention on the words you are saying. This is attention training — another essential skill for taking back control of your mind.

This tool is a very basic reprogramming of the subconscious mind, which is the next essential step if you are going to take full responsibility for everything that happens in your life.

About the Author

Kate Howells has been a counsellor for 10 years. She did her placement when training in an agency specialising in working with domestic abuse. She then provided counselling in a school for girls aged 11–18. Following this, she was Project Lead of a Victims of Crime Counselling Service for 13–25 year-olds. She now works solely in private practice, seeing individuals and couples on Zoom or Face-Face.

From the start of her counselling career, she found that she worked with a lot of clients who were autistic and/or had ADHD. She also specialises in working with clients who have experienced narcissistic abuse.

In more recent years, she has found that whilst counselling is really effective, many people also benefit from a more directive approach. Due to her own life having improved from resetting her subconscious mind, she has added this into the way in which she works.

Visit Kate's website: https://katehowells.co.uk

Email: info@katehowells.co.uk

Other Books and Services by the Author

This is Kate's first book! She is due to start writing her second one soon, and it will be about neurodivergence.

Contact Kate at info@katehowells.co.uk to enquire about individual or couples' counselling.

One More Thing Before You Go…

If you enjoyed reading this book or found it useful, I'd be very grateful if you'd post a short review on Amazon.

Your support really does make a difference, and I read all the reviews personally, so I can get your feedback and make this book even better.

If you would like to leave a review, then all you need to do is click the review link on Amazon here:

Thanks again for your support!

Bibliography

Freud, S. (1929). Civilisation and its Discontents, accessed 20 October, 2024
https://www.goodreads.com/quotes/146488-most-people-do-not-really-want-freedom-because-freedom-involves

Hosein Alavi, M. & Bulut, S. (2021). Reading Trauma as an Intergenerational Phenomenon, accessed 9 November, 2024, https://academicstrive.com/OAJBSP/OAJBSP180058.pdf

Miller, A. (1987). The Drama of Being a Child. Reprint. London: Virago, 1997.

Dyer, W. (2013). 'Dr. Wayne Dyer and the orange juice metaphor', accessed 20 October, 2024, https://www.youtube.com/watch?v=Fo7XPf9j9Io

The Brain from Top to Bottom. (n.d.). *Hierarchy of the three brains*. McGill University. https://thebrain.mcgill.ca/flash/i/i_05/i_05_cr/i_05_cr_her/i_05_cr_her.html

'Amygdala and Emotional Learning in Vertebrates - A Comparative Perspective', accessed 20 August, 2024, https://www.intechopen.com/chapters/41591

Barrett, L.F. (2017). How Emotions Are Made. Reprint. London: Pan Books, 2018.

Steffen, P.R., et al. (2022). 'The Brain Is Adaptive Not Triune: How the Brain Responds to Threat, Challenge, and Change', accessed 1 September 2024, https://www.frontiersin.org/journals/psychiatry/articles/10.3389/fpsyt.2022.802606/full

Schwartz, R. (2021). 'No Bad Parts', accessed 2022, https://www.audible.co.uk/pd/No-Bad-Parts-Audiobook/B0CKC6QR7F

Peters, P. S. (2012). The Chimp Paradox. Vermilion

Sadghuru (2021). Karma: A Yogi's Guide to Crafting Your Destiny. India: Penguin Random House.

Colier, N. 'Can't stop thinking: how to let go of anxiety and free yourself from obsessive rumination'. Oakland: New Harbinger, 2021.

Tolle, E. (2011). Where do our thoughts come from?, accessed 20 October, 2024, https://www.youtube.com/watch?v=rWFVi1cPUZo (Eckhart Tolle)

Hanson, R. (2020). The Brain: Teflon for the Good, Velcro for the Bad, accessed 27 October, 2024, https://www.youtube.com/watch?v=BwPvynau2oY

Ram Dass & Gorman P. (1985). How Can I Help? Stories and Reflections on Service. New York: Alfred A. Knopf

How the pain-body affects relationships, accessed 27 October 2024,
https://www.youtube.com/watch?v=5jSpDZVM1WE (Eckhart Tolle)

BBC Archive (1961). Aldous Huxley on the power of TECHNOLOGY! [Video]. You Tube. In Conversation, Classic Interviews, accessed 27 October, 2024,
https://www.youtube.com/watch?v=ZCOGFSwrGNc

Durvusula, R. (2024). It's Not You. How to Identify and Heal From Narcissistic People. London: Penguin Random House.

Evans, P. (1992) 'The Verbally Abusive Relationship'. Reprint: London: Adams Media, 2010.

Kernberg, O. F. (1975). *Borderline conditions and pathological narcissism.* Jason Aronson.

Cain, N. M., Ansell, E. B., Simpson, H. B., & Pinto, A. (2015). Interpersonal functioning in obsessive-compulsive personality disorder. *Journal of Personality Assessment*, 97(1), 90–99.

Theoryhttps://www.simplypsychology.org/charles-cooleys-looking-glass-self.html.

Very Well Mind (2024). ADHD and Toxic Relationships, accessed 1 October 2024 @ https://www.verywellmind.com/adhd-and-toxic-relationships-6831288

Marshall, A. G. (2006) 'I love you but I'm not in love with you'. London: Bloomsbury

Masters, R. A. (2013). Emotional Intimacy: A Comprehensive Guide for Connecting with the Power of Your Emotions. Boulder: Sounds True.

Little, M.A. (2023). 'Childhood Narcissism: A Guide to Preventing Narcissistic Development Before it Begins'. Maryland: Rowman & Littlefield

Durvasula, R. (2024), [June 18]. The Narcissism Doctor. '1 in 6 People are Narcissists! How to Spot Them and Can They Change?" Mayim Bialik's Breakdown. YouTube accessed 13 January 2025 @https://www.youtube.com/watch?v=A2mvGTQjQgk

Ram Dass (2015). Becoming Nobody https://www.amazon.co.uk/Becoming-Nobody-Essential-Dass-Collection/dp/1683646266

Sartre, J.P. (1943). 'Being and Nothingness' London: Routledge, 2003).

Hawkins, D. (2012). 'Letting Go', Hay House 2012

Stanford Graduate School of Business (2014, April 29) *Oprah Winfrey on Career, Life, and Leadership* [Video]. YouTube. https://www.youtube.com/watch?v=6DlrqeWrczs

Sadghuru (2020). *What is true love? A deeper insight*, Isha, accessed 2/11/2024

https://isha.sadhguru.org/en/wisdom/article/what-is-true-love

Maltz, M. (1960). Psycho-Cybernetics, Reprint: London: Souvenir Press, 2022

Ramm Dass (2014). Polishing the Mirror (Rameshwar Das) Audiobook. Audible.

Hay, L.L. 101 Best Louise Hay Affirmations of All Time. Accessed 10/11/2024,

https://www.louisehay.com/101-best-louise-hay-positive-affirmations/

Grimes, T. (2017). Simple Self-Healing Taught by Émile Coué. Cambridge: Amazon

Coué, É. (1922). *Self mastery through conscious autosuggestion*. Moffat, Yard and Company

Tim Grimes. 'The Law of Attraction Explored'

https://open.spotify.com/show/1uhuJ2u4xdrQl8xXc165HT?si=f13a452d8141475d

Murphy, J. (2007). The Power of Your Subconscious Mind. USA: BN Publishing (Original work published in 1963)

Krishnamurti, J. Krishnamurti on Meditation. Accessed 10/11/24

https://kfoundation.org/meditation/

Dodson, F. (2014). Parallel Universes of Self. Audible: Frederick Dodson

Goddard, N. (1956). Seedtime and Harvest. Neville Goddard, The Complete Collection (2023) USA: Fabio Mantegna

Hebb, D. (1949). Cited in Hebbian Learning (2020). Accessed 17/11/24, https://www.sciencedirect.com/topics/psychology/hebbian-learning

Goddard, N. (1968). I Remember When (with discussion) Brian Scott, accessed 23/11/24

https://www.youtube.com/watch?v=Vmx9C9iS6kA

Dodson, F. (2019). Deep Relaxation in 10 Minutes. Accessed 17/11/24 https://www.youtube.com/watch?v=SWIM5Mpok4Y

Hay, L.L. (2016) Mirror Work: 21 days to heal your life. Hay House Inc.

Adams, R. (2006). Silence of the Heart: Dialogues with Robert Adams. Acropolis Books.

Timeless Knowledge (2022). Dr Joseph Murphy: How to Manifest Your Best Life Accessed 18 December 2024 @ https://www.youtube.com/watch?v=Qyp_-yHsvCY0

Goddard, N. (1949). Out of This World. Neville Goddard, The Complete Collection (2023) USA: Fabio Mantegna

Golas, T. (1972) The Lazyman's guide to Enlightenment. California: Bantam Books (1981)

Dotts, R. (2016) Dissolve The Problem. Amazon.

Printed in Dunstable, United Kingdom